Tapping In

ALSO BY LAUREL PARNELL

Books

EMDR in the Treatment of Adults Abused as Children

A Therapist's Guide to EMDR: Tools and Techniques for Successful Treatment

Transforming Trauma—EMDR: The Revolutionary New Therapy for Freeing the Mind, Clearing the Body, and Opening the Heart

Audio

Tapping In: A Step-by-Step Guide to Activating Your Healing Resources through Bilateral Stimulation

LAUREL PARNELL, PH.D.

Tapping In

A STEP-BY STEP GUIDE TO
ACTIVATING YOUR HEALING RESOURCES
THROUGH BILATERAL STIMULATION

SOUNDS TRUE
Boulder, Colorado

DISCLAIMER

Although anyone may find the practices, disciplines, and understandings in this book to be useful, this book is made available with the understanding that neither the author nor the publisher are engaged in presenting specific medical, psychological, or emotional advice. Nor is anything in this book intended to be a diagnosis, prescription, recommendation, or cure for PTSD or any other specific kind of medical, psychological, or emotional problem. Each person has unique needs, and this book cannot take these individual differences into account. Each person should engage in a program of treatment, cure, or general health only in consultation with a licensed, qualified physician, therapist, or other competent professional. Any person suffering from PTSD or clinical depression should consult a doctor or licensed psychotherapist before practicing the exercises described in this book.

Sounds True, Inc.
Boulder, CO 80306

© 2008 Laurel Parnell

SOUNDS TRUE is a trademark of Sounds True, Inc.
All rights reserved. Published 2008.
Printed in Canada on paper recycled from 100% post-consumer waste
and processed without chlorine.

Cover and book design by Rachael Tomich

ISBN 978-1-59179-788-3

Library of Congress Cataloging-in-Publication Data

Parnell, Laurel, 1955-

Tapping in : a step-by-step guide to activating your healing resources through bilateral
stimulation / Laurel Parnell.

p. cm.

ISBN 978-1-59179-788-3 (softcover)

1. Eye movement desensitization and reprocessing. I. Title.

RC489.E98P35 2008

616.89'16—dc22

2007040958

DEDICATION

CONTENTS

Part Three:
More Resources & Resource Ideas

INTRODUCTION

This identity, out of the one and into the one and
with the one, is the source of and fountainhead
and breaking forth of glowing love.

—MEISTER ECKHART

SO MANY TRAUMATIC EVENTS have taken place in the last few years: hurricanes, tsunamis, war, and terror attacks, just to name a few. We may have experienced traumas ourselves or know someone who has felt their impact. Seeing images of people running from gigantic waves, people stranded on the roofs of submerged houses, and children dirty and crying beside bombed-out buildings can easily make us feel distressed and powerless. Most of us are also stressed trying to balance work and family life. Large numbers of us have difficulty sleeping, and many of us find ourselves taking medication or herbs to calm our frazzled nerves. In our troubled, anxious times there is a need for tools that can help us cope as well as find our way back to balance. The good news is that there are simple things that can be done to help, practices that can be easily taught to just about anyone with access to his or her own imagination. Some of those techniques can be found in this book—techniques that have been used successfully all over the world, with people of all ages, economic circumstances, and educational levels.

For the past sixteen years I have been practicing, teaching, and writing about Eye Movement Desensitization and Reprocessing (EMDR), a powerful and effective therapy for treating trauma, as well as an EMDR-related technique known as "resource installation." EMDR resource installation, or what I am calling here "resource tapping," is a method to strengthen and integrate internal resources so that we can call on them when we need them.

Resources include a wellspring of positive emotional memories and experiences, products of our creative imaginations that evoke feelings and essential qualities that are helpful to us. We all have resources within ourselves, such as memories of comfort and safety, experiences of being powerful and courageous, or images that evoke a feeling of peace and calm. These memories, qualities, and images are stored in our body-mind network and can be accessed, activated, and strengthened with bilateral stimulation by physically tapping on the body. This is called "tapping in" the resource. Then, for example, when anxiety strikes, you have created a shortcut to the resources you need to regain a sense of control and relaxation. I have found the resource tapping technique to be very helpful to my clients. I have used it to help them manage anxiety, lift their spirits, sleep better, increase their self-esteem, inspire creativity, and enhance performance.

The inspiration to write this book came a year ago when I was teaching EMDR at Esalen Institute in Big Sur. I had just seen Peter Levine make a moving presentation of his Somatic Experiencing® work with children who had been traumatized by the tsunami in Sri Lanka. Using simple methods of focus on bodily sensations, he was able to alleviate their suffering. He had just published a new book describing some of these methods for working with traumatized children. As I watched his slides, I thought about my own experiences with EMDR and EMDR resource work. Over the years I had witnessed thousands of people in my trainings and clinical practice experience relief from anxiety and trauma. I reflected that some of the simplest resource techniques using positive imagery and tapping could also provide quick relief from emotional distress following a traumatic incident.

My mind wandered to a conversation I had had with a colleague a few months before. A dedicated teacher and

EMDR practitioner, he had been traveling to the Thai-Burmese border several times a year to help Burmese refugees, who number in the millions. He told me that he was teaching refugees simple techniques that were having a dramatic effect on their level of suffering. Although his goal there was to teach EMDR to mental health professionals, he lacked the time and resources to do so. He had only enough time to teach them the most basic tools. Working through an interpreter, he had instructed the people to imagine a place where they felt safe and peaceful. Next he asked them to tap on their knees alternately—right-left, right-left—a few times. The tapping, a form of the bilateral stimulation used in EMDR, was meant to strengthen the positive feelings and to enhance the imagery. This very simple exercise yielded surprising results. Not only were these traumatized people able to imagine safe places and tap themselves back into positive emotional states, but they experienced a significant decrease in their level of anxiety and distress. Many of them reported no longer feeling traumatized by their experiences. Upon hearing his story, I thought that if I could get information out to the general public about some of the simple and easy-to-use EMDR resource tools, many people could be helped. What if some simple exercises that involve imagination and tapping could be taught that would help people find peace and inner strength? The more I contemplated it, the more enthusiastic I became. I have witnessed firsthand in my clinical practice, trainings, and consultation work how people have benefited from tapping in their resources. It dawned on me that much of the resource work can be easily taught to adults and children alike and doesn't necessarily require spending time (and money) in a therapist's office.

Driving back home up the spectacular Big Sur coast, the outline for this book began to form in my mind. When I got home I asked my colleagues what they thought of the idea, and they all supported it enthusiastically. They, too, believed that this information should be made accessible so that anyone could make use of it.

I have been in clinical practice since 1979, working with all kinds of people but specializing in the treatment of trauma. Along with my clinical work, I have been a spiritual practitioner most of my life. I was drawn to spiritual quest as a child and met my spiritual teacher, Lama Thubten Yeshe, in 1975. A Tibetan lama, he taught me about Buddhism and practices that involve contemplation and visualization of different deities. These deities represent aspects of our own enlightened mind. By imagining these deities and evoking their positive qualities, we awaken that which is latent within us, and we can manifest those qualities in our lives in a skillful way. Lama Yeshe embodied that which he taught: compassion, wisdom, power, and equanimity. He taught me about the deepest resource that is present within all of us—that which he called our "Buddha Nature."

When I was in my early twenties, Lama Yeshe gifted me with a direct experience of this inner resource. I had just spent the day with him and two friends visiting a sacred lake in the Sierras, where he did a ceremony to protect the lake with a group of Native Americans. We had taken him to a house where he was to stay for a few days before returning to a meditation retreat we were all attending. As I was walking down a hallway of the house, I encountered Lama Yeshe; immediately my heart overflowed with love for him. Yet I felt a little awkward, as I was also in awe of him—his presence was so powerful. Breaking the silence, I began to express my appreciation for him, but he stopped me. Taking my right hand in his, he gently but firmly placed it over my heart. Then, looking directly into my eyes, he said, "The Buddha is within you, dear." In that moment, time stood still. His words struck a chord of truth that resonated in the depth of my being. Tears streamed down my face. Truth recognized itself and came to the foreground of my awareness. The Buddha in me recognized the Buddha in him. I realized in that instant that we were not two, but one and the same. He held my gaze for a few moments then released my hand and continued down the hall.

Though Lama Yeshe passed away in 1984, I feel his presence very strongly in my life today. He was one of the first Tibetan lamas to teach Buddhism to westerners. He believed in simplifying the traditional visualization practices, finding their essence, and making them accessible to everyone. He wanted to bring the real meaning of Buddhism to everyday people in what he called "universal education." Much of what is presented in this book is influenced by Lama Yeshe and reflects what I learned over the nine years I knew him.

Jack Kornfield and Joseph Goldstein, who taught me Vipassana meditation in 1976, have also been important teachers and influences. For a period of ten years, I sat at least two eight-day silent retreats with them each year. In the late 1980s, I met Jean Klein, an awakened master of Advaita Vedanta. Over the next ten years, Jean helped further my spiritual unfolding. You will find elements of his nondual philosophy throughout this book.

Resource tapping is a modern psychospiritual method that echoes the spiritual technology of Tibetan and other meditative traditions, and is also influenced by hypnotherapy, guided imagery, positive psychology, and EMDR. All of these strands combine to provide a powerful and effective method for harnessing the power of the resources latent within us.

My hope in writing this book is that you will be able find the resources you need within the storehouse of your own being and derive sustenance from these resources that will enable you to accomplish your goals. I offer you many different tools that can be used in a range of situations, according to your needs. You can try these techniques on yourself or use them to help a loved one.

How to Use This Book

The chapters that follow teach you how to access your own resources and put them to use. In Chapter 1 I explain the basic principles of resource tapping that will guide your work. In Chapter 2 specific instructions are given on how to tap in resources, and Chapter 3 explains the four most commonly used resources. In Part Two of the book, I discuss a variety of practical situations in which the techniques can be applied, from managing anxiety to boosting creativity. Part Three lays out the many different types of resources we can access, with instructions for tapping in each one. The resources are organized into categories according to what they can do for you: provide comfort or refuge, bring peace and calm, empower you, lift your spirits, and inspire wisdom or help you connect to your spiritual resources. Once you are familiar with the basic resources, you can refer to the Table of Contents or the complete list of resources in the Appendix for resource ideas that will help you with a particular problem you are experiencing.

Part One

THE RESOURCE TAPPING TECHNIQUE

CHAPTER 1

Resource Tapping—
Origins and Principles

There is in all things an inexhaustible sweetness
and purity, a silence that is a fountain of action
and joy. It rises up in wordless gentleness and flows
out to me from unseen roots of all created being.

—THOMAS MERTON

MARYANN WAS SCHEDULED for surgery to remove a nonmalignant tumor from her breast. This was the second time she had developed tumors in her breast, and the second surgery. Because of how awful she felt from the general anesthesia after the first surgery, she wanted to avoid using it for this one. She asked her doctor if she could remain awake during the surgery. She told him that she would try to control her anxiety herself using a technique she had learned. She assured the doctor that if she became overwhelmed with anxiety she would agree to being put under.

The day of the surgery MaryAnn was anxious but determined to control her anxiety. As she was wheeled into the operating room, her heart beat loudly in her chest, reverberating like a drum. The nurses and techs were busy preparing the room, and the bright overhead lights glared down at her on the table below. The nurses prepped her for the surgery. They extended her arms out to each side and fastened her wrists to the table. She was immobilized, her body in the shape of a cross. The anesthesiologist gave her a shot so that she would not feel any pain during the surgery but gave her nothing for anxiety.

Surrounded by doctors, nurses, and techs, the bright lights exposing her bare breasts, MaryAnn's heart began to race. Her chest was tight, and it was hard to catch her breath. But in spite of her surroundings, she closed her eyes and brought her attention to a quiet, familiar place inside herself. She spent a few moments following her breath, feeling her body, being present. At first she attempted to keep herself calm by using her breath alone. When that didn't work, and waves of anxiety began to crash over her, she began to tap her fingers very lightly on the operating table— right-left, right-left. As she did this she noticed that the tightness in her chest began to release, and her breathing became smooth and flowing. She tapped for a while, stopping when she felt relaxed. She rested in a peaceful state for several minutes. Then her mind became active, and her chest began to tighten again. She began to tap her fingers once more, continuing until she once again felt peaceful and calm. Throughout the surgery, whenever she felt anxiety beginning to build, she would resume tapping. By the end of the surgery, she felt relaxed and at ease. She felt refreshed, not wiped out by the experience like the time before. She had done it! She was happy and proud of herself. This experience gave her confidence that she could get through other challenging experiences in the future with her resource tapping technique.

Our Natural Resources

Within each of us is a hidden potential, a wellspring of untapped natural resources we can use to heal our psychological wounds and help us better navigate challenges we face in our lives. The problem is that these resources too often remain buried, and we don't know how to access them. We dig in the wrong place, or we don't think to dig at all. Spiritual traditions teach ways to contact our resources by using prayer and meditation practices. Tibetan Buddhism, in particular, has developed sophisticated technologies for developing and cultivating different states of consciousness. Today, in western psychology, we have found a highly effective new way to harness the power of our inner resources. The technique is very simple. Sometimes I still find it hard to believe that it works, even though

I have experienced it myself, witnessed it work with my clients, and heard reports from my trainees and consultees. It sounds too easy to be possible.

This method, called "Resource Tapping," evolved out of Eye Movement Desensitization and Reprocessing therapy, or EMDR. EMDR, which was developed by psychologist Francine Shapiro in the late 1980s, is a powerful, well-researched treatment for trauma that incorporates alternating bilateral stimulation into a structured therapy. Shapiro found that people could process a trauma memory at an accelerated rate when it was paired with bilateral stimulation. People who had been suffering with post-traumatic stress disorder would find their symptoms relieved after only a few sessions. In the early days of EMDR, we used eye movements exclusively for bilateral stimulation. Clients were instructed to follow the therapist's fingers with their eyes, moving them to the far right and then far left. The eye movements used in EMDR were found to activate an accelerated processing effect. Clients would experience a mind-body free-associative processing during which emotions, body sensations, images, memories, and thoughts moved rapidly through their systems. Some well-regarded brain researchers believe that the bilateral stimulation used in EMDR may be activating both hemispheres of the brain much in the same way that REM sleep does. During REM sleep, our eyes move rapidly back and forth, and we process and integrate information.

But many people were not able to use the eye movements in EMDR. Some had eye injuries, were blind, or found it physically uncomfortable. Over time we discovered that other forms of bilateral stimulation also worked, as well if not better than eye movements, to elicit the accelerated processing effect. We began to tap on clients' knees and hands or to use alternating sounds, stimulating each side alternately—right-left, right-left. In this way we would activate each side of the person's brain, which seems to be the key to the rapid processing effect we see in EMDR.

When clients activate a disturbing memory by evoking the emotions, body sensations, and thoughts associated with it, and then add bilateral stimulation, they begin an extraordinary free-associative process between mind and body. Clients can have thoughts, feelings, old memories, or dreamlike fantasies that move rapidly through their awareness. As this information is processed, they often have new insights and new ways of viewing themselves and their lives. By the end of an EMDR session the old memories no longer feel disturbing. Clients naturally arrive at a place of health and wholeness.

Experience with thousands of people led to the foundational EMDR theory that within each person is a natural ability to heal that is disrupted after a traumatic experience. In this theory, our body-mind has a natural information processing system that works to process and assimilate new information. We have experiences all the time that are stored for later use. However, trauma memories are processed in a different way. When we have a trauma our information processing system is disrupted. The information is left in fragmented form, unprocessed, and not stored in long-term memory. The unintegrated fragments often cause symptoms that disrupt our lives. A sound or even a smell that reminds you of the trauma can elicit a full-blown panic response. Unprocessed traumas can cause us to feel anxious and depressed and to have nightmares and trouble sleeping. Instead of feeling like the trauma happened in the past, it feels like it is alive in the present. When you have a wound, your body cannot heal until the wound has been cleaned of debris. In the same way that debris inhibits our bodies' ability to heal, a serious trauma disrupts our natural healing system. The bilateral stimulation we use in EMDR activates our inherent information processing system and allows our minds and bodies to find their way back to wholeness.

In the early days of EMDR we discovered that bilateral stimulation could also be used in a focused way to activate and strengthen certain resources within our clients. The first resource to be tapped in was the safe place. Guiding people to imagine a place where they feel safe and comfortable had been used for many years by psychotherapists to help people reduce anxiety. We found that directing clients to focus on a safe place and then adding short sets of bilateral stimulation worked even better than the imagery alone to calm them and provide them with a sense of control over their distress. This practice, called "installing a safe place," helped traumatized people feel safer and was used by therapists prior to beginning EMDR sessions. Later we found that we could tap in many different kinds of resources—such as images of nurturing figures, protector figures, and inner wisdom figures—to help strengthen and stabilize clients who had been severely traumatized in childhood. Resource tapping became an important tool in helping to prepare clients for the difficult EMDR trauma processing work.

Over the years resource tapping has expanded and developed considerably. There are many positive resources that can be tapped in that comfort us, lift our spirits, or empower us, including inherent qualities such as love, wisdom, and joy, as well as memories, experiences, images that arise from our imaginations, and people to whom we can connect. Moreover, tapping in has expanded beyond EMDR and trauma work. Resource tapping is now done as a stand-alone technique, independent of EMDR, and new applications for resource tapping are being discovered every day. Resource tapping is used to reduce anxiety and depression, help with sleep, increase creativity and performance, aid in healing, and decrease distress after a traumatic incident. Colleagues of mine in Germany are using it to help cancer patients cope with their illness. School children with heavy course loads are using resource tapping to help alleviate their daily stress. By focusing attention on our resources and adding short sets of simple bilateral tapping, we can strengthen these resources, making them more present and accessible to us.

Resource tapping is related to EMDR but is essentially a different model. With EMDR we focus on the trauma memory, add bilateral stimulation, and follow a protocol that allows the unfolding of a free-associative processing. In contrast, when we tap in resources we focus on the positive resource and only allow a short amount of bilateral stimulation. We keep the work focused exclusively on the positive, healing resources and do not allow a free flow of processing. The idea with tapping in resources is that we want to select the resources according to the situation. We are using the resources as specific tools for specific applications. For example, if I am feeling anxious, I want to tap in resources that will help me relax. I might choose a calming image such as a verdant meadow covered with bright yellow flowers, a bubbling brook, and gentle grazing deer. As I bring my imagination to bear, and really see, smell, and hear this meadow, I tap right-left, right-left to increase the experience of relaxation this resource evokes in me. I do not allow myself to tap for too long. If I do, I risk activating anxiety-producing information.

Throughout this book I use the terms "tapping" and "tapping in" resources. We *tap in* a resource by locating the best one and using our imagination to activate it. When the resource is activated, we use tapping (bilateral stimulation) to strengthen and integrate the resource more fully into our system. When I refer to "tapping" here, I mean tapping alternately right-left, right-left, softly drumming on your knees, thighs, or the sides of your legs. You can also cross your arms in front of your chest and alternately tap each shoulder—as though hugging yourself—in what is called the "butterfly hug." Or you can alternately tap your toes or feet.

It is important to understand that resource tapping is not taking something from outside ourselves and putting it in; rather, we use this method to enhance resources that are already within us. Resource tapping has been very helpful for many people. It has become a wonderful tool to help reduce anxiety, cope with trauma and illnesses, sleep better, and increase confidence, among other things. Over time, a wealth of applications for tapping in resources has been developed, many of which I will share in this book. Resource tapping is something that can easily be done on your own, without a therapist.

Six Basic Principles

EMDR founder Francine Shapiro developed a theory she called "adaptive information processing" to explain the individual's movement toward health. I have expanded her theory here with my "basic principles." These are my own formulation, which evolved out of clinical experience using EMDR and resource tapping, Buddhist and nondual spiritual philosophy, and the perspective and insight I have developed from over thirty years of spiritual practice. I have been awed countless times working with clients who are able to use bilateral stimulation to discover their inherent wholeness. Spiritual experiences are quite common for EMDR clients, as well as for clients tapping in their resources. I was so inspired by the spiritual experiences of my clients that I wrote an article for the *Journal of Transpersonal Psychology* about my observations and my theories about why this might be occurring. Based on this article, research was conducted by a doctoral student who found that many other EMDR therapists were also reporting their clients having transpersonal/spiritual experiences during their sessions, confirming my observations. The following basic principles form the foundation upon which resource tapping is built. When you understand and experience these principles for yourself, you will be able to use the technique creatively in any number of ways.

1. We are essentially whole. This wholeness is our true nature. The expression of our wholeness is wisdom, compassion, equanimity, power, and joy.

2. Within each of us is the potential to realize this wholeness. Indeed, this wholeness wants to be realized, impels us to realize it.

3. We also have within us a reservoir of positive stored experiences. These can include experiences of loving and being loved, and of feeling comforted, competent, powerful, happy, joyful, peaceful, and calm.

4. We become unhappy when we are not able to access our wholeness, our reservoir of positive experiences, or when we are out of balance.

5. We have a natural healing system that, when accessed and activated using bilateral stimulation (tapping), can restore us to balance.

6. We can access, strengthen, and integrate our wholeness and our reservoir of resources by tapping in our resources.

PRINCIPLE 1

We are essentially whole. Wholeness is our true nature. There is an abiding presence that is never touched by what happens to us. Like the sun obscured by clouds, it remains shining in the background. Upsetting life events and our interpretations of these events are like the clouds that obstruct the experience of our wholeness, our true nature. Like sunlight breaking through the clouds, every once in a while we get a glimpse of our true nature; we feel a sense of something much larger than the small "me" we tend to identify with.

The expression of our wholeness is wisdom, compassion, equanimity, power, and joy. We have moments in life when we are able to express ourselves freely, when there is a natural flow of expression that springs from our deepest selves, our place of wholeness. We feel this love when we hold our children, and there are times when words of wisdom issue forth from our mouths that we didn't know we had. We feel empowered because we are coming from our ground of being. When we are in our fullness, we feel an expansion in our bodies, our hearts are open, and we feel joyful. Creativity is also an expression of our wholeness. In these moments, when we are momentarily free from the inner critic, we are more able to access whatever our creative gifts happen to be.

PRINCIPLE 2

Within each of us is the potential to realize this wholeness. Indeed, this wholeness wants to be realized, impels us to realize it. This drive toward health, wholeness, and freedom comes from our highest source. Deep within us is the desire to be free from the constraints of identification with the false self. All that isn't our true self is experienced as contractions in the mind and body. When I believe that I am my problems, or that I am any of the negative things I say about myself, I feel small, tight, and unhappy. When I recognize that I am so much more than my inner critic says I am, I feel free. We naturally know and recognize freedom. We are drawn to it. When we are blessed with glimpses of our true nature, we crave more. It is our wholeness that desires to be realized. We feel this drive especially strongly when we are spiritually oriented. Then our lives can become harmonious, and we can live in such a way that this wholeness comes to know itself more fully, unfolding like a flower.

PRINCIPLE 3

We also have within us a reservoir of positive stored experiences. Positive experiences create a feeling of expansion in the body and mind. They open us to life's possibilities rather than contract us and create limitations. Memories of feeling safe, loved, comforted, happy, joyful, awed, inspired, powerful, courageous, and peaceful are stored inside us. Everyone has positive memories and experiences. Even if you have had a terrible childhood, you have had times that were not fraught with trauma. Simple pleasures like petting your cat, feeling the warmth of the sun on your face, or enjoying a good meal are stored in your warehouse of experiences. There may be one person who was kind to you growing up, such as a neighbor, teacher, or grandparent, whose loving care is a memory upon which you can draw.

These positive memories are stored in memory networks. Webs of associations radiate from key life experiences. The strands that make up the webs can include images, emotions, body sensations, sounds, smells, tastes, and beliefs. An example of a positive resource memory could be an experience of baking cookies with your grandmother as a child. You have the *image* of yourself as a child with your grandmother baking in her kitchen. You *smell* the cookies baking. You *taste* the sweet, delicious cookie batter and then the soft, warm cookies. You *feel* the warmth in the kitchen. You *hear* the sound of the beater and your grandmother's voice. You *feel* comforted, happy, and loved. Later in life, when you think of your grandmother's cookies, you feel warm inside. The smell of cookies baking may make you happy, lighting up the network where these pleasant memories reside.

The problem is we don't pay as much attention to these positive experiences as we do to negative ones. We tend to focus on what is lacking rather than what is working well. For example, I have a lovely Chinese watercolor in my office. In one corner of the picture there is a tiny tear in the paper that only I seem to notice. This flaw keeps me from seeing the picture as a whole and enjoying its beauty. Likewise, we may focus on what we see as flaws in ourselves rather than appreciate our strengths. In spite of our tendency to focus on the problems, our good qualities remain inside us as potential resources that we can access and integrate into our broader view of ourselves and our world through resource tapping.

PRINCIPLE 4

We become unhappy when we are not able to access our wholeness, our reservoir of positive experiences,

or when we are out of balance. Life events and our interpretation of those events can throw us off balance and trigger feelings of fear, anxiety, and depression. We can criticize ourselves for not feeling or doing better. This, of course, makes us feel worse. For example, if I have had painful and distressing experiences with medical professionals in the past, I might dread a visit to the dentist. I might feel vulnerable, powerless, and unsafe. As the dentist approaches, I might find myself sweating, feel my heart start to beat rapidly, and want to get up and run out the door. In that moment I am not accessing my reservoir of experiences of when I felt safe and powerful in the past. Instead I am cycling in the repository of scary medical experiences. I tell myself I'm stupid for feeling so afraid, this is a nice dentist, but my negative self-talk is not comforting; instead, it reinforces feelings of shame and the belief that there is something wrong with me for being nervous.

Unpleasant experiences can create life-limiting memory networks. These networks can dramatically affect how we view ourselves and our world in the present because we create a sense of self from our interpretations of experiences. For example, if as a child you were shamed by your parents for wetting your bed, you may come to believe it isn't safe to fall asleep. Your body may hold the memory of the humiliation and loss of control, but on a conscious level you may not have any idea why you have problems falling asleep. The experience may be over, but the story your memory network has created about it continues to run your life. This negative view of yourself may then be reinforced throughout your life when you experience other humiliations.

PRINCIPLE 5

We have a natural healing system that, when accessed and activated through bilateral stimulation (tapping), can restore us to balance. When we experience anxiety or distress of some kind, if we tap alternately right-left, right-left on the knees or shoulders, it can help to calm us. This is what happened for MaryAnn during her surgery.

Despite all the empirical evidence of the power of bilateral stimulation to help people in the ways I'm describing here, we do not know how it works in scientific terms. There are theories that may shed some light on the mechanism. One possibility is that the rhythm of the stimulation causes a calming effect on the nervous system. For thousands of years cultures all over the world have used drumming and dancing to process traumatic experiences. It is possible that the calming effect rhythm has on us is simply hardwired into the human nervous system from the time we were in our mother's womb, floating in a safe, calm environment, and heard the rhythm of our mother's heart. Perhaps the sound of her heartbeat then became linked in our developing baby's body-mind to the feeling of calm, to which the rhythm now reconnects us.

On the other hand, some brain researchers believe that the processing effect of EMDR's alternating, bilateral stimulation is a result of constantly shifting attention across the body's midline. This process of alternating attention is similar to what happens during REM or dream sleep. These researchers believe that the alternating bilateral stimulation causes the activation of memories and their integration into a broader contextual understanding. Brain scans have demonstrated that activating both sides of the brain helps facilitate the processing of information. Research has also shown us that alternating bilateral stimulation is more effective than stimulation on both sides simultaneously.

Rhythm and bilateral stimulation do seem to be inherently soothing to the nervous system. We instinctively rock and pat a baby when it cries. When you are upset, and go for a walk, don't you feel better afterward? Is it the bilateral stimulation of stepping left and right, or is it the rhythm of the walking that is having the effect? We don't know, but I suspect that they both play a role.

PRINCIPLE 6

We can access, strengthen, and integrate our wholeness and our reservoir of resources by tapping in our resources. Our imagination is very powerful.

Techniques that use imagination and visualization are used to heal physical and psychological problems in many forms of therapy. Brain research has shown that when we imagine doing something, neurons in the brain are activated as if we were actually doing it. For example, if you imagine moving your right arm, the same region of your brain is activated that would be if you were actually moving your arm. Clinical experience has shown that tapping strengthens this activation even more.

We are going to explore many resources in this book and learn how to access them with our imagination. When you imagine a resource that you want to cultivate—such as peace, joy, love, or power—you can bring to mind a memory of when you experienced it, an image that evokes it, or someone or something that represents it for you. Activating your imagination in this way, in its greatest capacity, brings in as many of your senses as possible and can be very powerful. The more detail you can bring to the visualization, the more vibrant the experience will be for you.

Let's say you want to feel calmer, more peaceful. You might begin by thinking of a time when you felt calm and peaceful. You remember a time you hiked up to a beautiful, clear mountain lake. You sat by the lake, which was surrounded by snowcapped mountains, and had a picnic lunch. As you ate your lunch you gazed out at the beauty around you and felt at peace. When you close your eyes and go inside, bringing up the memory as strongly as you can, you *see* yourself sitting by the lake. You *hear* the sound of water gently lapping against the shore and the wind in the trees. You *feel* the crisp mountain air and a cool, refreshing breeze. You *smell* the pines and lake. Your body relaxes; you feel happy and peaceful. When you can strongly feel these peaceful feelings, you have activated the resource you wish to tap in. You have used your imagination to locate the stored positive information.

When your resource has been activated, when you have a strong feeling for it, you add the tapping. You tap a short time—6 to 12 times, right-left, right-left. The tapping helps you to feel the resource more fully in every way. Using your imagination brings it up, but the tapping does something more. Even though we only tap for a very short duration of concentrated resource activation, the effects last far longer than the actual moments of tapping. In fact, the resource experience seems to move more fully into the body.

Tapping in our resources seems to help assimilate them into our whole experience of ourselves, making these resources more accessible to us. Tapping in seems to integrate memory networks. When we tap right-left, right-left, we help the brain process and integrate information that is stored in different compartments. Imagine a large house with many rooms. Only a few rooms are used on a daily basis, many of the best rooms are rarely used, and some are entirely forgotten. When we bring our focus to resources we wish to cultivate and then tap them in, what seems to happen is that the doors to the forgotten rooms open and are made accessible to the rest of the house. Instead of just using a few rooms, more of the house is available to you.

With this understanding of the six basic principles, we can begin to identify, cultivate, and enhance the resources that are most beneficial to us. In the chapters that follow, I will provide you with specific instructions on how to tap in resources, descriptions of the most commonly used resources, and how to use resources for many types of problems. In the last part of the book I will provide you with more resources you can tap in and ideas for their practical application.

Definition of Terms

Bilateral Stimulation The use of eye movements, tactile sensations, sounds or physical movements to stimulate the left and right hemispheres, or sides, of the brain. Bilateral stimulation is used to activate and integrate information from these two hemispheres.

Resources Inherent qualities such as love, wisdom, strength and joy, as well as memories, experiences, mental images, or people to whom we can connect. Resources reside within us.

Activation Bringing a resource into consciousness through your imagination so that all of your senses are alive and its qualities are available to you.

Tapping Using the hands to alternately tap (right-left, right-left) on the knees, legs or shoulders in order to achieve bilateral stimulation. Other methods include alternately tapping your feet on the floor or simply tapping any surface with your fingers.

Resource Tapping / Tapping In Resources

A technique that pairs an activated resource with alternating bilateral stimulation via tapping to strengthen and integrate the resource. For example, in order to tap in the resource of peaceful place, you would imagine a place where you feel a sense of peace, such as a verdant park. When you can imagine the park and feel the peacefulness, you tap for a short period of time, strengthening and integrating the feeling of the resource so that it becomes more easily available.

CHAPTER 2

Tapping In Your Natural Resources

Keep knocking, and the joy inside
will eventually open a window
and look out to see who's there.

—RUMI

Imagination: The Essential Tool

Tapping in your resources is relatively easy to do. As we've discussed, it begins with your imagination. You might want to begin by tapping in one or more of the most commonly used resources: safe/peaceful place, nurturing figures, protector figures, and inner wisdom figures. In Chapter 3 I will explain what these are and how to tap them in. By tapping in the most commonly used resources, you will be preparing a resource tool kit that you will have available to use when you need it. It is like having your basic household tools in a handy place where you can find them and use them to repair things that are not working in your home. These resources will be your basic tools to help you feel less anxious when flying, driving, speaking in public, or taking tests, and to help you sleep better, perform more optimally, recover faster from trauma, and enhance your body's ability to heal.

You begin by imagining the resource, evoking as much of the sensory information as you can in order to feel the desired qualities. When you feel your resource is well-activated, you begin to tap it in. For instance, as I'll describe in the next chapter, you can imagine your safe/peaceful place. When you have activated the image, feeling, and sensory information, you add tapping to strengthen the associations and integrate the information into your current situation. After tapping in a safe/peaceful place, you might then think of nurturing figures and tap them in. You can continue in this way with all the resources you wish to collect in your basic resource tool kit. By doing this, you will know what your resources are and will be able to activate and tap them in when you need them.

Once you've completed the initial tapping-in process and established your resources—your safe/peaceful place, your nurturing figures, and so on—you can call on these resources when the need arises. When you find yourself with a problem or in a difficult situation, ask yourself what quality or resource would help you. For example, if you are anxious, you might want a resource that is comforting or calming. You can then imagine one of the resources you have already tapped in, such as your safe/peaceful place. When you have the resource well-activated through visualization, and can feel its quality, you can begin tapping. You may think of another resource, and tap that in as well. There are innumerable resource ideas to choose from, many of which are found in later chapters. If you prepare yourself by identifying your resources, you'll know what to do when a problem arises.

There are two times when you tap in resources: first, when you are not in a situation of immediate need, as a way of identifying and locking in your resources in order to have them ready when you *do* need them; then, later, at a time when you need to bring in specific resources for specific applications. In the first instance basic resources such as safe/peaceful place, nurturing figures, protector figures, and inner wisdom figures are tapped in. These resources can then be more easily imagined and tapped in at a later time when their help is needed. For example, if you are feeling anxious about a dental visit, you might want to imagine your safe or peaceful place and nurturing figures, and then tap them in. Resources that haven't been tapped in before can be elicited and tapped in, too. For example, if you are nervous about making a speech, you might want to recall a time when you felt confident and successful speaking, and then tap in that memory.

When tapping in a resource, it is important to use your imagination to enhance your sensory experience of the resource as much as possible. You have to feel the resource in your body. Just thinking about it is not enough. When you bring it to mind, be sure to notice what you are you seeing, feeling, smelling, tasting, and hearing.

For example, one way to elicit the resource of love is to think of someone you care for. Bring an *image* of the person to mind. If you have difficulty visualizing, *imagine* the person through whatever images or sensations arise. We create mental images all the time without realizing it. You don't have to "see" an image of the person in perfect detail to access the power of the resource. What is most important is that you have the feeling of the resource you are evoking. Let's say you are going to tap in your best friend, whom you love. When you think of her, what do you see? Perhaps you imagine her sweet, smiling face. As you imagine her face, what do you feel?

Sometimes it is easier to find the resource by locating a specific memory. Do you have a memory of her that could help in this particular instance? Maybe recently you went out to lunch with her and had a caring, connected conversation, during which you felt seen, heard, and understood by her. Now, as you imagine your friend, let yourself feel your love for her. Feel your heart becoming soft and warm. When you can feel the quality you are trying to elicit, you have the resource activated. This is when you begin to tap.

Tapping In: Basic Practice

Tapping in your resources can include many forms of alternating bilateral stimulation. You can tap on your legs or knees, like drumming. You can lift your feet and tap them on the floor or march in place. It is important to tap one side and then the other. In this way you will be stimulating each side of your brain. You can also do the butterfly hug. For the butterfly hug, cross your arms in front of your chest and alternately tap each shoulder. The butterfly hug is helpful to use when you want to feel comforted.

The following steps are the most basic approach to tapping in resources. In the course of this book, we will discuss many variations of the technique, but this is the method that serves as the starting point and foundation of this practice.

1. Find a comfortable place to sit or lie down where you will not be disturbed. Turn off the ringer on your phone, or do whatever else you need to do to prevent distractions.

2. Close your eyes. Bring your attention to a quiet, still place inside yourself. You can begin by taking long, deep breaths and slowly exhaling. Relax and release with each exhalation. Alternately, use the Grounded Breathing practice included in this chapter.

3. Bring to mind the resource you have chosen to work with. It can be a positive memory, an inherent quality, an experience, or an important person or animal.

4. Imagine the resource as fully as you can. Open your senses. Notice what you are seeing. Notice what you are hearing. Notice what you are smelling. What sensations do you feel on your skin? What do you taste? What do you feel inside? Take the time you need to elicit this information and fill out the resource.

5. When you have a strong sense of the resource, when you can feel its quality, begin to tap on your knees, right-left, right-left; or do the butterfly hug, crossing your arms in front of your chest and alternately tapping on each shoulder. Tap 6 to 12 times, then stop and check in with yourself. If it feels good, and the resource is strengthening, you can tap some more.

6. Tap as long as it feels positive. If other memories or resources come to mind that feel good, you can tap them in also.

Begin to tap at a slow, rhythmic pace, and then find the pace that feels best to you. While you tap, focus on the whole feeling the resource evokes in you, allowing the feeling to increase. At first, tap for only a short time—alternating right-left, right-left, approximately 6 to 12 times. After one round of tapping, stop and check in with yourself. What are you experiencing? If the resource is strengthening, tap some more. You may continue tapping as long as it remains positive. Some people prefer longer rounds of tapping. This is fine as long as the resource remains positive.

Many people can only do a few right-left taps before they begin free-associative processing that can take them far afield. For example, sometimes a positive memory resource will flip to the negative or become contaminated in some way. In the middle of tapping in the memory of a loving interaction with your grandfather, your mind might flash on a loved one who is angry with you. For this reason, it is best to do short sets and see how you are feeling. With practice you will learn what works best for you. As with most things, you'll get better at tapping in your resources with practice.

If you've found yourself tapping in a resource that is not entirely positive, you should stop tapping immediately and try one of the following techniques. Test out any or all of these, to see what works best for you.

- After you have stopped tapping, see if you can think of another, different resource that is fully positive. *It is important that the resource feel completely positive.* If you can find another one, tap it in, this time tapping for a shorter duration.

- If a distressing memory has arisen, you can imagine placing it in a container that can hold it for you. You can imagine this container as anything that can safely hold the material that has come up. You might imagine a safe, a vault, or a treasure chest with a good lock. It is important that the container have a strong lid. This imagery can help you consciously compartmentalize information that is too much to integrate in the moment. It is a skillful way to handle material that does not feel manageable. (Later, if you choose, you can take the material out of the container and work on it.) Once you feel the memory is sufficiently contained, you can return to the resource you began with or bring up another one that has only positive feelings and associations. This time tap for a very short time—just 4 or 6 taps, right-left, right-left.

- You can imagine returning to your safe/ peaceful place, one of the primary resources that I describe in Chapter 3.

As I mentioned in Chapter 1, when tapping in your resources you must be careful that you do not activate the reprocessing of traumatic memories. Tapping can cause your mind to connect to and light up all kinds of old memories, including ones that are distressing. *If you have a lot of trauma in your background, be very careful with the tapping in of resources.* Do very short rounds of tapping, proceeding cautiously. Be sure to stop and check in with yourself before continuing with more tapping. You may want to consult with an EMDR therapist to reprocess your trauma memories prior to tapping in resources on your own. This book is a guide to creating support for your mind and body, but is not a substitute for psychotherapy. If disturbing information should arise that you have trouble dealing with, seek professional help.

Resource Tapping at a Glance

1. Find a place where you won't be disturbed.

2. Go to a quiet place inside yourself, using techniques such as Grounded Breathing.

3. Bring to mind your resource memory, experience, imagination, or figure.

4. Activate the sensory details of that resource until they are alive.

5. Begin to tap right-left, right-left 6 to 12 times. If the resource is continuing to strengthen and feels positive, you can continue to tap.

6. If you wish, you can tap as long as
the resource remains positive.

---

* **Grounded Breathing Instructions**

Find a comfortable way to sit so that your back is
straight but relaxed and your feet are uncrossed and
resting on the floor. You may also sit cross-legged
if you wish. Close your eyes and be aware of how
your body feels. Notice the places of contact . . .
your bottom on the seat and your feet on the floor.
Be aware of your breathing. Where do you feel it?
What is its rhythm? Now imagine that as you inhale
a deep, full breath, you are taking the air from deep
within the earth. This breath comes up through your
legs and fills your belly . . . then your chest . . . and
now your throat. When you feel the breath in your
throat, hold it a moment, then exhale, letting the air
leave the throat . . . then the chest . . . and now the
belly . . . releasing the air back down into the earth.
When the need arises to take another breath, again
breathe in from the earth, filling your belly, chest,
and throat . . . pause, and then slowly exhale, throat,
chest, belly, back down into the earth. Let the air
fill your body. Let the inhalation, and exhalation be
gentle and smooth. Be aware of the sensations in
your body. If your mind wanders away, gently bring

it back to the breathing. Smooth and gentle. Be
present. The goal is attained moment to moment.

CHAPTER 3

The Four Most Commonly Used Resources

This morning's mine,
the ruby sun rising.
gold streaking the horizon,
the emerald bay still, waiting,
no human cry disturbing,
this morning's mine.

—JEAN PUMPHREY

IN THIS CHAPTER I will introduce you to the four most commonly used and accessible resources: safe/peaceful place, nurturing figures, protector figures, and inner wisdom figures. These resources can be easily summoned and tapped in for many kinds of problems or situations. Most people can access these resources. By locating and tapping in these resources before you need them, you are consciously developing and placing these most important and useful tools where you can find them. If you need more help than these four basic resources provide, or simply want more resource tools in your tool kit, you will find many more ideas in Parts Two and Three of this book.

In EMDR treatment many therapists begin by helping their clients tap in these four basic resources. When this has been done, the therapist and client know that they have the basic resources necessary to handle stressful situations if they arise. Tapping in these essential resources creates a foundation of safety and stabilization for the work.

Safe / Peaceful Place

The safe/peaceful place is a resource you can develop and tap in so that you can calm yourself and reduce anxiety. It is one of the resources used most often for this purpose. The safe/peaceful place is somewhere you feel safe and protected. It can be a known place, or it can be an imaginary place. Many people choose a place in nature, such as a beautiful beach or mountain lake. It can also be symbolic, such as in the arms of a large mother bear or in a warm, cozy cave. In developing the safe/peaceful place, you want to create a place of self-nourishment, safety, and comfort where you can relax. For some people, the purpose of the safe/peaceful place is to help them relax and feel secure, whereas for others the emphasis is more on finding a sanctuary where they can contact their wisdom and creativity. You can imagine going to your safe/peaceful place as a means of self-soothing, and you can even use it before going to sleep at night. The safe/peaceful place can also be a place where your allies gather to add extra safety and support. (This will be described in more detail later in this chapter.)

Safe/peaceful place imagery has been described and used by many people. Simply imagining a place that is safe and comfortable can be powerful in and of itself. However, combining imagination and tapping serves to strengthen the imagery more fully, integrating it into the nervous system and making it more accessible and useful. I have heard many stories of people tapping and imagining their safe/peaceful places during times of distress to help create a feeling of calm. People in countries all over the world, rich and poor, young and old, have used this resource. Children can be taught to tap in their safe/peaceful places, too.

If you have been traumatized or are anxious and stressed, you may want to focus even more attention on making your safe/peaceful place feel secure. If you feel the need for extra safety, you can imagine putting a protective barrier around your safe/peaceful place. You might imagine a protective shield around it, like something out of Star Trek, or imagine fierce protectors guarding it. For some people the word "safe" immediately evokes associations to its opposite, "unsafe." People who have had many experiences of being unsafe may begin to think about those experiences when the word "safe" is used. If this is true for you, don't call it "safe" place, use "peaceful," or "comfortable" instead. It is most important that you locate and activate imagery that relaxes and calms you.

At the beginning of the safe/peaceful place experience, you want to enter a state of general relaxation. Some people can contact an image and feeling of a peaceful place easily, while others require more preparation. The time necessary for relaxation depends on how you are feeling in the moment. It is important that you are able to feel relaxed as you evoke the safe/peaceful place imagery.

 ## Tapping In Your Safe / Peaceful Place

1. Find a comfortable place to sit or lie down where you will not be disturbed. Turn off the ringer on your phone, or do whatever else you need to do to prevent distractions.

2. Close your eyes and go inside. Do the grounded breathing practice from Chapter 2 or use another method to calm yourself, such as progressive relaxation, or mindfulness meditation, and come to the present moment.

3. Once you are relaxed, imagine a place where you feel safe and comfortable, a place where you can feel peaceful and relaxed. (If desired, use the Safe/Peaceful script.)

4. After finding the place, enhance it using your senses: What do you see? What do you hear? What do you smell? What do you feel?

5. You can choose to reinforce the feeling of safety by erecting a protective barrier or adding protectors to guard your safe/peaceful place.

6. When you have a strong positive feeling, begin to tap. Tap 6 to 12 times, right-left, right-left.

7. You can tap longer, as long as the tapping continues to strengthen your experience of the safe/peaceful place in a positive way.

8. If you feel distress or experience the intrusion of negative imagery, stop tapping immediately. As discussed in Chapter 2, extended tapping opens up processing of distressing material for some people. If this happens, stop the tapping and explore what you are experiencing. You may need to develop another safe/peaceful place using imagery only. You may also want to use the word "comfortable" or "peaceful" instead of "safe," as previously mentioned.

9. You can use a cue word as you tap in the safe/peaceful place. For example, if your safe/peaceful place is a beach, you can imagine the beach with the associated feelings of relaxation and say to yourself "beach" as you tap. When you do this, the cue word becomes linked with the feelings of relaxation and comfort that your safe/peaceful place evokes. During times of anxiety or distress, you can invoke the safe/peaceful place imagery with the cue word. For instance, if you have to make a speech and are anxious, you can say the word "beach" and imagine your safe/peaceful place to elicit a feeling of calm.

10. Remember this is *your* safe/peaceful place. You can contact it whenever you would like. All you have to do is close your eyes and imagine your special place. You can repeat your cue word to yourself as you imagine your safe/peaceful place and tap to access and strengthen your connection to it.

USING A PEACEFUL PLACE DURING AN ANXIETY-PRODUCING FLIGHT

When Cynthia flies, which she does frequently for work, she tries to make sure she gets an aisle seat. Because she feels trapped and uncomfortable, she doesn't like to sit by the window or in the middle seat. She wants to be able to get out of her seat easily and walk around. On a recent trip to the East Coast, she had an aisle seat on the first leg of the trip and assumed she would have one for the next leg. But when she changed planes, she discovered she had been assigned a middle seat. To make matters worse, her seat was between two very large men. Cynthia is a small woman, a little over five feet tall, and she felt like sandwich filling sitting between those two men. Finding herself in this predicament, she thought, "What am I going to do?" Scanning the rows, she saw that the plane was completely full, every seat occupied. She realized that she would not be able to change her seat. There was nothing she could do about it. Fortunately, the men sitting beside her were friendly, and the flight was only two hours long. Cynthia thought that she would be able to make it through.

Then, not long after takeoff, they hit large pockets of turbulence. The plane bucked up and down like a bronco, and Cynthia gripped the armrests as her stomach lurched, twisting in knots. As the turbulence continued, her anxiety climbed. She felt claustrophobic and trapped, with a strong impulse to flee.

Cynthia wanted to get control over herself. She did not want to have a panic attack. She remembered her resource tools and decided to tap in her safe/peaceful place. She closed her eyes and went inside herself, imagining herself at a favorite beach. She imagined that she was standing in the warm ocean on a sunny day. Visualizing the beach and feeling the relaxation she associated with it, she began to tap on her knees, right-left, right-left. As she tapped she began to imagine that she was jumping up and down in the ocean waves. The turbulence became the rolling waves of the ocean she was playing in. She began to calm down. She felt lighter, even happy. She continued to tap the entire time the plane was turbulent and felt very relaxed. There were several episodes of turbulence on the flight. Each time one started, she would close her eyes and imagine herself playing in the ocean waves and tap. In this way she was able to calm herself down and even enjoy the ride.

Script for the Safe / Peaceful Place

THE FOLLOWING IS A GUIDED IMAGERY SCRIPT
TO YOUR PEACEFUL PLACE. YOU CAN READ THIS
AND RECORD IT, HAVE SOMEONE READ IT TO
YOU, OR REMEMBER IT AND GUIDE YOURSELF.

Find a comfortable way to sit so that your back is
straight but relaxed, and your feet are uncrossed and
resting on the floor. You may also sit cross-legged if you
wish. Close your eyes and be aware of how your body
feels. Notice the places of contact . . . your bottom on
the seat and your feet on the floor. Be aware of your
breathing. Where do you feel it? What is its rhythm?
Now imagine that as you inhale a deep full breath,
you are taking the air from deep within the earth. This
breath comes up through your legs and fills your belly
. . . then your chest . . . and now your throat. When
you feel the breath in your throat, hold it a moment,
then exhale, letting the air leave the throat . . . then
the chest . . . and now the belly . . . releasing the air
back down into the earth. When the need arises to take
another breath, again breathe in from the earth, filling
the belly, chest, and throat . . . pause, and then slowly
exhaling, throat, chest, belly, back down into earth. Let
the air fill your body. Let the inhalation and exhalation
be gentle and smooth. Be aware of the sensations in
the body. If your mind wanders away, gently bring

it back to the breathing. Smooth and gentle. Be present. The goal is attained moment to moment.

Imagine yourself in a peaceful, relaxing place. This place can be real or imaginary. It might be somewhere you've been before, from a dream or fantasy you have had, somewhere from a movie or book, or somewhere you have heard about. Let the image of the place come to you . . . this place that is peaceful, calm and serene . . . a special inner place for you . . . somewhere you feel at ease . . . a place where you feel safe and secure. It can be a sanctuary, somewhere to go to be quiet and reflective . . . somewhere special and healing for you. When you have found your safe/peaceful place, let yourself explore and experience this place as if you were there now. Notice what you see there. Notice what sounds you hear. What do you smell? Notice what it feels like to be there. Allow yourself to absorb the feelings of peacefulness . . . of being secure and at ease. Immerse yourself in serenity.

When you can sense and feel the peacefulness of the safe/peaceful place, you can begin to tap. Tap a few times and allow the feeling of relaxation to increase. If you feel good you can tap longer, as long as your place continues to feel safe and comfortable to you. Spend as much time as you would like in your safe/peaceful place. Keep tapping as long as you feel relaxed and peaceful.

When you feel complete, the safe/peaceful place well-established, tell yourself you can return to this place anytime you wish. This special place of safety, relaxation, and serenity is always available to you. If you would like, you can choose a cue word that will help you to remember your safe/peaceful place. As you say the cue word to yourself, tap to link it to your special place. In the future you can say this word to bring back the feelings of your safe/peaceful place.

USING ART TO ENHANCE YOUR SAFE / PEACEFUL PLACE

Art can be used to create or enhance the safe/peaceful place. Drawing the safe/peaceful place can give it more substance for you. This is your special place, and you can make it any way you wish. When you draw, the connection to it may strengthen, and you can add details to your picture to make it even more secure.

If you have difficulty finding a safe/peaceful place, you can draw a "safe island." The safe island is drawn on a large piece of paper. Find a piece of paper large enough for you to stand in the middle of, like butcher paper. Stand in the center of the paper, and draw a large circle around yourself. This is your safe island. Create your safe island any way you would like. You can draw anything and anyone you want on the island. Make it as safe and peaceful as you want. If you would like, draw a protective barrier around the island or protect it with guardians.

Even when it is easy to imagine a safe/peaceful place, some people find that their sense of comfort increases when they draw it. Afterward, you can use your drawing as a reminder of your safe/peaceful place to help you feel calmer and at ease.

✳ Tapping In Your Safe / Peaceful Place Through Drawing

1. Get a piece of blank paper, and use markers, crayons, pastels, or any other drawing utensil.

2. Close your eyes and go inside. Imagine a place where you feel safe and secure, a place that is serene and peaceful.

3. When the image comes to you, begin to draw it. Don't censor yourself or judge your artistic skills. Just allow what comes to be expressed on the page. It is most important to create some kind of visual representation, even if it looks like a drawing a child would make. What do you need to make it as safe as you would like?

4. When you have completed the drawing, take a look at it, and take in the feelings it evokes. Add whatever else you would like to it, even guardians to make it more protected.

5. Close your eyes and hold the image in your mind. Now begin to tap. Tap right-left, right-left, 6 to 12 times. Continue to tap as long as it strengthens your positive feelings.

Nurturing Figures

Who comes to mind when you think of someone or something that could nurture and care for you? Did your grandmother hold you in her arms when you were a child and make you feel safe and secure? Did you have a favorite dog that comforted you when you needed it? Do you have a close friend who makes you feel cared for? Who you know who would be there to help you in a time of need? Have you been soothed by an angelic being? These nurturing resources can be tapped in and made available to calm and comfort us. Nurturing figures can include real or imaginary figures from the present or past, inner guides, and even animals. Look for those people from your past who were loving, safe, nurturing figures for you. There may be a parent or stepparent, sibling, grandparent, nanny, aunt or uncle, teacher, coach, doctor, counselor, friend's parent, or clergy person who was an important source of caring for you. There may be people from your current life who are important resources for you, such as a spouse, friend, or lover. Figures from movies, TV, or books, historical figures, or people from popular culture can be used as nurturing resources. Mr. Rogers, Mary Poppins, and the fairy godmother in Cinderella are examples of resources people have used. Spiritual figures can also be used as nurturers, including Mary, Jesus, a Native American elder, an angel, or one of the Buddhist goddesses, like Kuan Yin or Tara.

Animals can be valuable nurturing figures. These can be pets from your present or past or animals for which you have a special affinity. Perhaps you have a dog or cat that comforts you, or you had one as a child. Growing up I had a large, long-haired black cat named Cinder whom I adored. He would sleep on my bed and follow my sister and me when we played outdoors. I remember cuddling with him and petting his soft fur during troubled times. His presence was always comforting to me.

You may have a spiritual connection with an animal or mythological creature (for example, a wolf, bear, lion, panther, coyote, eagle, or dragon). In Native American spiritual traditions these are power animals, allies or guides that carry a sacred quality. Your power animals can be tapped in and then called upon for nurturing, advice, and protection.

Your adult self can be used as a nurturer, too. See if you can connect with your innate qualities of nurturing and compassion. Have you been able to love someone or something? You can contact your nurturing adult self by recalling times in your life when you cared for another. Remember holding your child in your arms or petting your cat. This quality resides inside of you, and you can activate it and tap it in to provide comfort and support when you need it.

If you have a history of neglect and meager nurturing it can be difficult to find nurturing figures. In this case you might think of someone you know who is nurturing to someone else. Perhaps you remember a friend holding her daughter and speaking kindly to her. You can bring to mind an animal caring for its young, such as a cat caring for her kittens. You can even use movie stars as nurturing figures. One client of mine came up with the actress Meryl Streep as her nurturing figure. She could imagine her as a loving mother who could provide her infant self with the love and attention she needed to develop in a healthy way.

The following are some of my nurturing figures: my grandmother, my grandfather, my husband, several friends, Lama Yeshe (my spiritual teacher), and my adult self. Many people find that having a combination of real people from the past and present as well as spiritual resources, such as deities or angelic beings, provides them with a greater feeling of support. They feel they have a whole team of loving allies. Also, there are times when one nurturing figure is more helpful to call on than another. It is useful to have many options available. For example, if you are facing a medical procedure, you may want to call on a loving figure from your childhood who can soothe the fears of your inner child self. The partner you have previously also tapped in as a nurturer may not be the best choice at that time if he or she is also anxious and in need of support.

When tapping in a nurturing figure, it is important to imagine the figure in its nurturing aspect. This can include memories or images of the figure being nurturing. For example, you might think of a time when your grandmother held you in her arms and sang to you. This image represents the quality of nurturing you are wishing to strengthen and make available. Your grandmother may also serve as a protector figure, but in that case you would tap in an image of her acting in a protective way.

✳ Tapping In Nurturing Figures

1. Spend a few moments going inside and quieting your mind.

2. Think of a figure from your present or past you associate with nurturing. This can be a person, an animal, a spiritual figure, or even someone from a book or movie. When you imagine the figure, *feel* the nurturing quality in your body.

3. After finding your nurturing figure, enhance the image as strongly as you can. What do you see? What do you hear? What do you smell? What do you feel in your body?

4. When you have a strong sense of the nurturing quality of the figure, begin to tap. Tap 6 to 12 times, right-left, right-left. Stop. Check in with yourself. How do you feel?

5. If the nurturing quality is continuing to strengthen, you can tap some more if you wish. Continue to tap as

long as you feel the figure and the nurturing quality strengthening and integrating.

6. If there is more than one resource, you can bring the next nurturing figure to mind, and then tap it in also.

7. Repeat this process, tapping in one resource at a time.

8. When you are through, you might want to imagine yourself being held by your nurturing figure or figures. As you imagine that, tap some more to strengthen and deepen the feeling of being nurtured.

✱ An Angel as a Nurturing Figure

THE FOLLOWING SCRIPT CAN BE READ
TO YOU BY SOMEONE ELSE, OR YOU
CAN RECORD IT FOR YOURSELF.

Close your eyes and go inside. Take a deep breath in, filling your belly, chest, and throat, hold it a moment, then exhale slowly, from your throat, your chest and your belly. Relax, let go with the exhalation. Now take another breath, take your breath in from deep in the earth, filling your belly, chest, and throat. Hold it a few moments . . . now exhale releasing from your throat . . . chest . . . and belly. Relax, let go. Let yourself settle into the present moment.

Now, imagine your angel hovering near you. You see her beautiful face emanating serenity and compassion. She has large silky, soft wings within which she can enfold you. Warm, golden light radiates from her being, filling you with a feeling of being nurtured and protected. Her very presence is relaxing. If it is difficult to see her, you can simply feel her presence as a warm glow all around you. This glow permeates your entire being. When the feeling of nurturing is strong, the quality well activated, use the butterfly hug and tap on either shoulder right-left, right-left several times. As you tap you can feel the nurturing quality of your angel strengthen. Imagine yourself enfolded in the loving wings of your angel. Stop tapping when it feels complete for you. Remind yourself that your angel is always there. All you have to do is imagine her and tap.

Protector Figures

Protector figures are allies you can summon in your imagination to give you strength and to help you feel protected. They can be used to reduce anxiety and to empower you. Protector figures can be real people or animals, or imaginary figures from books, movies, TV, or dreams. A protector can be someone from your child-hood or from your present life. You might choose your protective adult self. It is most important that when you think of your protectors that you can feel that they would defend you against harm. Who would protect you if you needed help? Who could you summon that is strong, powerful, and protective? Who would watch your back?

If you can't think of a real person, is there someone from a movie or book?

Many people choose animals as protectors. They can be pets or even power animals. One of my clients had a powerful tiger ally who served as her protector, while another client chose a hawk. Spiritual figures from many traditions can be used, including protective angels and deities. Memories of positive interactions with real-life protector figures can also be tapped in. You might find that the figure you use for nurturing also serves as a protector. One woman's dragon served as a protector, nurturer, and wise figure. Examples of protector figures people have used include parents and grandparents; friends; partners and spouses; dogs, cats, elephants, or horses; one's protective adult self; movie actors who play strong action heroes like Bruce Willis and Arnold Schwartzenegger; and superheroes or mythic figures like Spiderman, Superman, Wonder Woman, Athena and Hercules; or even the genie Mr. Clean!

When you tap in your protector figure, it is important to imagine the figure in its protective aspect. For example, if the protector is your friend, imagine your friend exhibiting protectiveness toward you. You want to *feel* the quality of protection from the figure. Sometimes it can be helpful to summon a memory of when the figure was protective of you, or if it is a figure from a book, TV show, or movie, a scene when the figure exhibited that quality.

✳ Tapping In Protector Figures

1. Close your eyes and go inside. Take a few moments to bring yourself to the present moment. You might take some deep, relaxing breaths. When you are feeling in the here and now, bring to mind someone or something from your life you feel would be protective of you. It can be someone you know from the present or past, an animal, or even a figure from a movie, book, or TV. It can be a spiritual figure that is protective, or it can be your adult protective self. You can have more than one figure. Now find an image that represents your protector figure. You want this image to represent your protector in his or her protective aspect.

2. Now when you imagine your protector, notice what you are seeing. What are you hearing? What are you feeling in your body? What emotions do you feel? Let your senses come alive.

3. When you have a strong feeling for your protector, begin to tap. Tap 6 to 12 times. Now stop. Check in. How do you feel? If the feeling or imagery of the protector is getting stronger, or you want to go longer, tap some more as long as it remains positive. Stop tapping when you feel your protector resource strong inside you.

4. Now if you would like, think of another protector. What image do you have that represents it? Again, activate your senses, really feeling the protector, and then tap to strengthen and integrate it.

5. Repeat the imagination and tapping of protectors as long as you would like.

6. Imagine yourself in the future using your protectors for support. Tap as you imagine it.

CIRCLE OF PROTECTION

You can increase the feeling of protection by imagining a circle of protection comprised of all your protector figures. This can be used during times when you feel vulnerable and afraid and wish to feel your protectors more fully.

✳ Tapping In Your Circle of Protection

1. Close your eyes and go inside. Take some deep breaths in, and slowly let them go. Relax with each exhalation. Bring yourself to a quiet place inside.

2. When you are relaxed, imagine yourself surrounded by your protector figures. Look around the circle. Look at each protector, one at a time. Feel their love and protection of you. If you like, you can enhance the details of the imagery and sense of protection. It is important that you feel the sense of protection from your protector figures.

3. When you have a strong sense of them, begin to tap. Tap 6 to 12 times. Stop and check in; if the feeling of protection is getting stronger, continue to tap. Take in the strength of your protectors. Let their courage in. Receive their determination to protect you.

4. You can also draw your circle of protection. Draw yourself surrounded by your protectors. Drawing can serve to reinforce the feeling of protection. Viewing your drawing can provide you with a sense of protection when you need it. You can also tap as you look at it.

USING PROTECTOR FIGURES TO HANDLE A CHALLENGING FAMILY SITUATION

Donna was feeling fragile and overwhelmed in her life. The holidays were coming up, and she was going to visit her family. Throughout her childhood her father drank heavily, exploding verbally with little warning. Though he had been sober for many years, whenever she was back home Donna felt anxious and powerless.

Donna wanted to feel prepared for the visit. In order to decrease her anxiety and feel more protected, she decided to tap in her protector figures.

She closed her eyes and took a few moments to focus internally. She then thought about who she could use as protector figures. Several came to her mind. She named her husband, her best friend, Kate, her dog, Toby, and James Bond (more specifically, James Bond as played by Sean Connery).

The first protector she brought up was her husband. As she imagined him in his "protector aspect," she felt the quality of protectiveness in him. She could feel that he would protect her in a time of need. When she could see him, and feel that quality in him, she tapped on her knees. She tapped for a short time, then stopped. She could feel the feelings well established. She then brought her friend Kate to mind. She thought of the protective quality in her and tapped to strengthen it. Next she thought of her dog, Toby. But when Donna thought of Toby and tapped, she began to feel sad. Toby had died a few years ago, and the tapping was bringing up memories of the loss. Because of these feelings, she was not able to use him as a protector resource at that time. She put aside the upsetting memories of her dog and focused her attention on her husband and friend with their protective qualities. When she could feel their protection again, she tapped a short time to strengthen it. Finally, she brought up the image of James Bond. She saw him, full of confidence, intelligence, and latent power, coolly confronting a bad guy. She tapped to strengthen that image and feeling. When she had tapped in all of her protectors, she felt much more confident. She even thought of others who might serve as protectors. She no longer felt alone with her difficulties.

THE PROTECTIVE ADULT SELF

Your adult self can also be a protector figure. This is the part of you that can be contacted to protect you or those you love. You can find the adult protective self by getting in touch with a number of skills and traits you already have inside, and then tapping to strengthen and integrate these qualities so that you can better contact them and harness them for use when you need them.

✳ Tapping In Your Protective Adult Self

1. Close your eyes and go inside. Take some deep breaths and slowly let them out. Relax and release with each exhalation. Bring yourself to the present moment. When you feel yourself present, see if you can find a time when you were protective. Can you think of a time when you defended someone you cared about? Be aware of whatever memory or image that comes to mind.

2. When you find the memory, notice what you see. What are you hearing? What do you notice in your body? When you have the image and can *feel* the quality of protectiveness, begin to tap. Tap 6 to 12 times.

3. Stop tapping and check in. How are you feeling? Can you feel the sense of protectiveness? If you wish you can tap again as long as the experience remains positive and the feeling of protectiveness strengthens.

4. Now think of a time when you were courageous. What picture comes to mind?

5. As you bring up the picture, notice what you feel. Notice what you hear, smell, sense. What do you feel in your body?

6. When you have the image and the feeling of courage strongly activated, begin to tap. Tap 6 to 12 times. Stop tapping and check in with yourself. How do you feel? If you want to strengthen the quality of courage further, tap some more.

7. Other qualities associated with protectiveness include strength, confidence, groundedness, and more. Continue to think of times when you felt these qualities and tap to strengthen and deepen them within you.

8. After you have felt all of these qualities within yourself, bring all of them together into a single sense of self.

9. Now tap to strengthen and integrate them. You might have an image that arises that represents the protective adult self. Let any image arise that feels like it captures all of the qualities of protectiveness that you have tapped. It is important that you have a bodily sense of the resource.

Inner Wisdom Figures

Inner wisdom figures are aspects of yourself that represent your inner wisdom. They can be very valuable allies, and after they have been tapped in, they can be called on in times of difficulty. The most important role of the inner wisdom figure is to *empower* you. Inner wisdom figures can also be present as a source of support and comfort. When you develop inner wisdom figures, you can gain a greater sense of connection to your own inner resources. Tapping in inner wisdom figures provides you with another tool, one that reminds you how to access your own source of wisdom and creativity. I know people whose inner wisdom figures have included fairies, wise men and women, grandfathers, grandmothers, trees, waterfalls, elves, wizards, religious figures, animals, Native American elders, goddesses, an older version of the person represented as white or golden light, their own wise voice without any image, and many others.

You can use your inner wisdom figures to help you in a number of ways. If you have a question or problem or don't know which direction to turn, take a moment and go inside yourself. Bring up your inner wisdom figure and ask him or her for guidance. Then tap—and listen for the response. In this way your inner wisdom figure can be there to provide guidance and support for you in your life. You may have more than one inner wisdom figure, and they may change each time you do the exercise. You may require a different inner wisdom figure for different problems in your life or at different times in your life.

Your inner wisdom figures come from your own source. They may be people you haven't known or even heard of before. In order to find inner wisdom figures, it is helpful to imagine going to your safe/peaceful place first. After you are in your safe/peaceful place, you imagine meeting your inner wisdom figure. Your inner wisdom figure will appear spontaneously. It is important that you let it appear in whatever form it takes. Sometimes you may be surprised at what comes, as the inner wisdom figure can take a variety of forms. It is important that you not judge what comes up for you. When you find the inner wisdom figure, ask its name. Accept what it tells you. When you have found the figure and have a name for it, begin to tap. Tap as long as it feels positive.

After the inner wisdom figure appears, and you have tapped it in, you can ask for any advice he or she has to give you. It is also important that you accept the advice your inner wisdom figure offers you, as long as it is compassionate. You then tap again. You can tap continuously as long as the information and associations remain positive. If the experience should become negative, stop tapping and return to your safe/peaceful place.

There are other wise figures you can use to help you that I describe in Chapter 17. These are wise figures you already know—teachers, spiritual guides, helpers that you have known personally or may have encountered in movies, on TV, or in books. What is described here, however, is a method to access inner wisdom figures that arise spontaneously when you are in a state of relaxation. Though they may be figures already known to you, these inner wisdom figures come from a place deep within you and are more closely associated with your own reservoir of inherent wisdom.

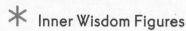

Inner Wisdom Figures

THE FOLLOWING SCRIPT CAN BE READ BY
SOMEONE TO GUIDE YOU, OR YOU CAN
READ IT AND RECORD IT FOR YOURSELF.

Close your eyes and go inside. Take a deep breath
in, filling your belly, chest, and throat; hold it a
moment, then exhale slowly, from your throat, your
chest and your belly. Relax; let go with the exhalation.
Now take another breath; take your breath in from
deep in the earth, filling your belly, chest, and throat.
Hold it a few moments . . . now exhale, releasing
from your throat . . . chest . . . and belly. Relax, let
go. Let yourself settle into the present moment.

When you feel yourself relaxed, imagine going to
your safe/peaceful place. This is your special place
where you are at peace, where you feel at ease. Take
as much time as you need to find this special place.
When you are there, notice what you see. Look
around. What sounds do you hear? What do you smell?
What bodily sensations do you notice? Go inside
yourself. How are you feeling in this special place?

As you relax in your safe/peaceful place or
sanctuary, invite your inner wisdom figure to join
you. Just allow an image to form that represents
your inner wisdom figure—a wise, kind, loving figure
who knows you well. Let it appear in any way that

comes, and accept it as it is. It may come in many forms—man, woman, animal, friend, someone else you know, or a character from a movie or book.

Accept your inner wisdom figure as it appears, as long as it seems wise, kind, loving, and compassionate. You will be able to sense its caring for you and its wisdom. Invite it to be comfortable there with you. Ask its name and accept what comes. When you have found your inner wisdom figure, begin to tap. Tap a few times, and see how you feel. If it feels good, you can continue tapping. If it feels bad in any way, stop tapping and return to your safe/peaceful place.

You may end here, or you may continue by starting a conversation with your inner wisdom figure, asking him or her questions and then listening for the answers that come.

To begin, tell your inner wisdom figure about your problem. Ask any questions you have concerning this situation. Now listen carefully for the figure's response. You may imagine your figure talking with you, or you may simply have a direct sense of its message in some other way. Allow it to communicate in whatever way seems natural. If you are uncertain about the meaning of the advice or if there are other questions you want to ask, continue the conversation until you feel you have learned all you can at this time.

As you consider what your inner wisdom figure told you, imagine what your life would be like if you took the advice you have received. If you have more questions, continue the conversation.

When it seems right, thank your inner wisdom figure for meeting with you, and ask it to tell you the easiest, surest method for getting back in touch with it. Recognize that you can call another meeting whenever you feel the need for some advice or support. Say good-bye for now in whatever way seems appropriate, and allow yourself to come back to the room.

===

USING AN INNER WISDOM FIGURE TO RECOVER FROM AN ACCIDENT

Annie was hit by a car while riding her bicycle on a country road. She was badly hurt, but thankfully her injuries were not life-threatening. During the course of her rehabilitation, she worried that she wouldn't be able to recover enough to resume her active life. The prospect of a long recovery dispirited and discouraged her. She realized it was important to connect more with a feeling of hope that would empower her to move forward in her physical therapy. She used resource tapping to help.

She closed her eyes and focused her attention inside. Then she called on her inner wisdom figure, her wise self. When she had a sense of it, she began to tap right-left, right-left, on her legs. As she tapped, she asked for guidance and support. Soon she began to hear, "We can do this no matter what." The words made her feel supported. She tapped more. She heard, "Even if you compete in the Special Olympics, you will regain an active life." She tapped for several minutes, feeling more and more supported by her inner wisdom figure. She realized that she would be okay and that she could get through it.

Later, throughout her recovery process, she would tap in her inner wisdom figure whenever she needed guidance or support. Her inner wisdom figure proved to be a helpful resource for her.

Your Circle of Inner Helpers

Now that you have tapped in your basic resource figures, you can imagine them together with you in your safe/peaceful place, surrounding you and providing you support. You can tap in this circle of helpers and fully take in the sense that you have a whole team of resource figures there to assist you. You can imagine taking your circle of inner helpers into your life. They can be called upon and tapped in to help you when you need them. As we explore other resources and resource figures through the rest of this book, you can add them to your circle of inner helpers as well.

✳ ### Tapping In Your Circle of Inner Helpers

1. Imagine yourself surrounded by your inner helpers. You are in the center of a circle of support. Take a

moment to look at each one of your inner resource figures. Feel their support for you. Take it in, feeling it as strongly as you can in your body.

2. Now feel the combined support from your inner helpers. Feel their caring and the qualities they provide as you tap in this entire team of inner helpers. When you can feel the sense of support strongly in your body, begin to tap. Tap as long as it feels positive.

3. While you tap, you may imagine more inner resource figures joining your circle. Some may arise spontaneously, adding even more support for you.

4. Imagine taking this feeling of support with you into your life. When you have an image, picture, or sense of doing this, tap to strengthen it.

5. Remember that your circle of inner helpers is always there. All you have to do is think of them and tap.

Having assembled these basic resources, you will be able to put them to work when you need them. They offer you a solid basis for exploring the many other resources described in Parts Two and Three.

Part Two

PUTTING THE RESOURCES TO WORK

CHAPTER 4

Managing Anxiety

Life shrinks or expands according to one's courage.

—ANAÏS NIN

EVER SINCE HER ACCIDENT, Audrey has felt anxious whenever she drives. She just can't trust that someone won't hit her. Evelyn hates going to the dentist. She feels so vulnerable sitting in the dentist chair immobilized, with her mouth wide open. Her anxiety prevents her from seeing the hygienist for regular cleaning. Bill experiences anxiety whenever he flies. Turbulence sets his heart racing and his palms sweating. He feels foolish gripping the armrests and praying that the plane won't go down.

There are many situations that create anxiety for us. We may feel anxious flying, driving, going to the doctor, dealing with family crises, speaking in public, or traveling to unfamiliar places. Anxiety is an awful feeling. We feel fearful, our bodies taken over by our rapidly beating hearts. Our breathing becomes shallow and we have the urge to flee. Anxiety often makes us feel like we don't have control over ourselves. Many people feel anxious because of traumas from the past. Like Audrey, after a car accident you may feel anxious driving or even being a passenger in a car. Some people who have had a lot of traumas experience anxiety about many things; they feel a general sense of being unsafe. There is even research indicating that there is a genetic predisposition to anxiety—some of us have nervous systems that are more prone to anxiety.

The National Institute of Mental Health conducted research that showed anxiety disorders to be the number one mental health problem among American women and the second most important problem among men. Nearly forty million people in the United States suffer from some kind of anxiety disorder, including panic attacks and phobias. We are living at a time in history when we are experiencing a great deal of stress. We are frequently moving at a rapid rate, working long hours with few vacations. We don't take the time to relax, unwind, and replenish ourselves. Since the terrorist attacks of September 11, some of us live with increased fear and uncertainty. Our use of technology also seems to add to our stress level. We are bombarded with information, overloading our systems with frequent use of our cell phones, computers, TVs, radios, and even old-fashioned newspapers. We multitask constantly—driving, talking on the phone, and eating, all at the same time. In the United States many of us eat on the go; we don't take the time to sit down and enjoy a meal with friends or family as is common in other countries. We are adrenaline junkies, getting a lot done but never seeming to catch up.

We may not be aware of it, but anxiety affects our entire systems. Our bodies react with rapid heartbeat, muscle tension, queasiness, dry mouth, or sweating. We feel apprehensive and uneasy. Extreme anxiety can cause us to have panic attacks or to dissociate, detaching from ourselves so that we feel like we are floating outside of our bodies. Anxiety affects how we behave. We may lose confidence in our ability to do things or face situations. It can impact our self-esteem and sense of self-efficacy.

Anxiety can be a normal response to a fearful situation, when you are waiting to hear from a doctor after a medical test, for example. Anxiety disorders differ from normal anxiety in that they are more intense, last longer, and interfere with functioning in our lives. This would be the case for someone who has been traumatized after an assault and is so fearful and anxious she cannot leave her house.

Tapping in your resources can be used to manage anxiety. If, however, your anxiety has developed into an anxiety disorder, I recommend that you seek professional help. EMDR can be very effective in treating anxiety disorders—especially post-traumatic stress disorder—and is available in many communities around the country (see EMDR Information at the back of this book). Those with more common forms of anxiety, on the other hand, can benefit greatly from the use of resource tapping.

Resource tapping can be used in many ways to help manage anxiety. You can even evoke and tap in your resources as a kind of regular meditation to help calm you and give your nervous system a rest. As mentioned earlier, we need breaks to let ourselves unwind. Taking time to access our resources and tap them in can help decrease our general stress level. Why not imagine your safe/peaceful place, complete with allies, before going to sleep at night or when you wake up in the morning? Take a break from work and imagine yourself at your special beach playing in the waves, and tap it in. By paying attention to our general stress level and tapping in our resources, we can feel calmer.

You can also tap in resources to manage your anxiety when it arises during specific situations—if you feel anxious driving, flying, going to the doctor, speaking in public, or meeting with your boss. You can use the resources from your tool kit you have already tapped in or find something that more specifically fits the situation you are dealing with.

Suggestions for Tapping In Resources to Manage Anxiety

When you feel anxious, ask yourself, "What do I need to feel less anxious? What resource would help me?" Then listen to what comes into your mind. The most commonly used resource to help manage anxiety is the safe/peaceful place. Imagining your safe/peaceful place and then tapping it in can often calm you. Perhaps you might want to use the nurturing, protective, and inner wisdom figures you have tapped in to help you. Here are some of the possible approaches you can take:

- Tap in resources that bring comfort: safe/
  peaceful place, sacred place, nurturing figures,
  spiritual figures, comfort memories, circle of
  love, memories of loving and being loved, loving-
  kindness meditation (see Chapters 3, 12, 13).

- Tap in resources that bring peace and
  calm: images from nature, memories of
  feeling peaceful, a resource person who
  brings peace and calm (see Chapter 14).

- Tap in resources that inspire wisdom and
  spirituality: inner wisdom figures, images of
  a wise being or higher power, your essential
  spiritual self, insights and life lessons, spiritual

teachings and wisdom resources, inner mentor or coach. An inner support team can be assembled and tapped in composed of all of your resource figures (see Chapters 9 and 17).

- If you feel that you need more power or strength, tap in resources for empowerment: protector figures, a circle of protection, core inner strength, power figures, courage, memories of saying no and setting boundaries, memories of saying yes (see Chapters 3 and 15).

- Sometimes repeating soothing, encouraging words to yourself while you tap can help to calm you.

If those don't feel like the right resources, or you need something more, look at the list of resource possibilities in the Appendix.

USING RESOURCES
TO MANAGE FEAR OF DRIVING

Audrey had been in a car accident that left her emotionally shaken but not badly injured. She was crossing an intersection when another car ran the red light and broadsided her. After the accident she became anxious driving. She felt that at any minute someone was going to hit her. She found herself constantly checking the rearview mirror to see if someone was too close. Though she realized her hypervigilance was actually making her less safe, she couldn't control it.

Before beginning EMDR sessions addressing the accident, I taught her resource tapping. Audrey learned to imagine a safe/peaceful place and to tap to strengthen the feeling of relaxation. She imagined a beach she loved with a broad expanse of white sand and warm gentle waves. She could see the pelicans flying over the water and could smell the salt spray. As she immersed herself in the imagery and feeling of her special place, she tapped on her knees. She found this worked well for her. After a few minutes of tapping her face relaxed, and she took a deep, releasing breath. She left the session with this tool to use whenever she felt anxious.

The next week she reported that she had been successful at calming herself before driving. She would imagine her safe/peaceful place and tap to reduce her anxiety. She did this several times throughout the week whenever she felt anxious. It worked so well for her that she felt herself in control of her fear for the first time in months. She felt happy that she had a simple tool that really worked for her.

USING RESOURCES TO GET THROUGH A DEPOSITION

Michael was a medical doctor who used resource tapping to get through a stressful deposition. He was being sued by a former patient who accused him of purposely causing her harm. Her unscrupulous lawyer was after as much money as he could get. Though Michael believed he had done nothing wrong, he was powerless to stop the suit. He had to endure the grueling, humiliating depositions leading to a possible court trial. During the first deposition, Michael became flustered, talked too much, and did not represent himself as well as he might have. But at the second deposition, Michael was better prepared. He had learned that he could take breaks when he was anxious and could tap in his resources.

After an hour of interrogation, the attorney was becoming successful at knocking him off balance, and Michael felt himself beginning to lose his composure. Recognizing this, he asked to take a break. He excused himself and retreated to the men's room where he entered a stall and closed the door. He sat down, closed his eyes, and brought his attention to his breath. He took some deep breaths and let go with a long exhalation. Then he imagined his safe/peaceful place. He imagined himself walking by a lake that he loved. He felt the sun warming his body, a slight refreshing breeze caressing his cheek. He could smell the water and the woods. He could hear the gentle waves, water birds, and chirping crickets. As he imagined this special place, he relaxed. Then he began to tap on his knees, right-left, right-left. He tapped as he continued to imagine himself at the lake. He was safe there, happy and peaceful. He let the feeling of well-being permeate his body, fill him, calm him. The tapping allowed the experience to become more fully integrated into his whole system.

After this, he brought up his protector figure—the boxer Rocky Balboa from the *Rocky* movies—and tapped him in. As he continued to tap, he thought of other protectors and power figures. He thought of times when *he* had felt powerful and tapped them in as well. As he tapped in these resources, his confidence increased; he felt larger, more capable. When he returned to the deposition, he felt calmer and more in control. Whenever he began to feel anxious, he discretely tapped his knees beneath the table and imagined his resources. From time to time he requested breaks during which he returned to the restroom stall and tapped in his safe/peaceful place and protectors. Several hours of intense questioning went by, but this time he was not shaken. He felt calm and in control throughout the experience. Because of his tapping, the lawyer was unable to throw him off balance. He left the attorney's office feeling good about how he had handled himself.

Tapping Alone Can Calm You Down

Using tapping without imagery is a way to reduce anxiety and calm yourself or a loved one relatively quickly and easily. As explained earlier, bilateral stimulation such as drumming, tapping, or dancing naturally soothes us, possibly reminding us of the beat of our mother's heart when we were in the womb. Bring your attention inward, and tap right-left, right-left, until you feel some relief. If you are a parent trying to calm a crying child, you can hold your child and tap gently on his or her arms or shoulders. When you do this, your child can better take in the support your holding provides. You can say comforting things to your child like, "It's okay, you're okay, it's over. You're with me now," and so forth.

If you feel anxious about speaking in front of a group, driving, crossing a bridge, or performing in some way, or you've just had a scary experience that has got your heart racing, you can tap to calm down. You can repeat encouraging words to yourself as well: "I'm going to be okay," or "I can do it," whatever you need to hear. Just tap right-left, right-left, alternately. If it helps, continue tapping. If for any reason you begin to think of something distressing, or if you feel more upset, stop tapping. Bring yourself back to the present moment. Find your breath. Take some deep, relaxing breaths, and exhale slowly. If tapping alone isn't working for you, you might want to tap in one of your stored resources.

✳ Tapping without Imagery

1. If it is possible, find a place to sit that is quiet.

2. Bring your attention to a still place inside yourself. Take some deep, relaxing breaths, and slowly let them out.

3. Begin to tap alternately, right-left, right-left, on your knees. If you are tapping someone else, such as a

child, you can tap his or her knees or shoulders or any-where that feels good to that person.

4. As you tap you can say comforting words.

5. Tap 6 to 12 times. Check in to see how you (or the person you're tapping) are feeling. If you are relaxing and feeling better, continue to tap.

6. Tap as long as it feels good.

USING TAPPING ALONE TO MANAGE ANXIETY ABOUT SWIMMING

Jane was anxious about swimming. She didn't have confidence in her ability to make it across the pool. She realized that her fear was irrational; she knew how to swim well enough to do it, but still her body began to tremble as she started swimming, and her confidence abandoned her. She made it one lap, but her heart was beating loudly. Remembering what she had learned from her therapist in session, she began to tap on her legs under the water, right-left, right-left. After just a short while she took a releasing breath and felt her anxiety vanish. She felt confident she could do it! She pushed off from the side of the pool and swam across with little effort. She continued to swim laps without any more difficulty.

Helping with Sleep

Nearly 30 percent of adults suffer from insomnia. We require good sleep in order to function and feel our best. Most people need seven to eight hours of sleep per night. Some of us have difficulty falling asleep, while others have difficulty staying asleep. There are many different things that can interfere with sleep, including too much caffeine during the day, lack of exercise, too much stimulation before bedtime, serotonin and/or melatonin deficiency, excess levels of stress hormones, irregular bedtimes, noisy partners, misuse of sleeping pills, and even worrying about falling asleep. These are all things that can be addressed through resource tapping. Tapping in resources can be used to help calm your mind and body so that you can fall asleep and can also be used to help you go back to sleep if you wake up.

✳ Tapping In Resources to Help with Sleep

1. Before going to bed, avoid caffeine, the nightly news, your computer, or anything else that will stimulate your mind or body. Take a bath, meditate, pray, do some yoga, or gentle stretches, or listen to relaxing music. Prepare yourself to let go.

2. When you get into bed, take some deep, relaxing breaths. Breathe up from the soles of your feet, filling your abdomen, chest, and throat with air. Hold the inhalation for a few moments, and then slowly release it, letting go from your throat, chest, and abdomen, deflating like a balloon. Take several of these deep, relaxing breaths.

3. When you feel calmer, bring to mind imagery that will relax you, with as much detail as possible.

You might imagine your safe/peaceful place, a sacred place, your nurturing figures, spiritual figures, or a pleasant memory. You may want to evoke resources that are comforting (Chapter 12), calming (Chapter 14), or spiritual (Chapter 17). You can create an imaginary scene that will relax and comfort you, such as being wrapped in the arms of a loving mother bear or in the wings of an angel.

4. Images or memories of letting go, expanding, or opening can be evoked. For example, you might imagine flying like an eagle, wings spread, soaring and free. Feel yourself letting go and expanding with the imagery.

5. When you have the resource well-activated, tap it in. You can cross your arms over your chest and tap your shoulders in a hug, or tap the sides of your legs. Tap as long as it feels good and you feel relaxed.

6. While you tap, you can add in more sensory detail, as long as it remains completely positive. For example, you can feel the softness of your mother bear's fur, feel yourself cuddling into her warmth, and hear the beating of her heart.

7. As you tap you can say calming words to yourself, such as "I can let go, I can relax, I'm done with my work, I can drift off to sleep."

8. You can sing yourself a lullaby in your mind. What lullabies touch your heart and soothe you? Are there lullabies from childhood that come to mind? Perhaps there is something you have heard more recently that

touches you? If Roy Rogers was a comforting figure to you as a child, for example, you might imagine him singing "Happy Trails." Tap until you let go into sleep.

9. If you should wake up in the night, tell yourself it's okay. Bring up your comforting images, and tap them in. Tap until you relax into sleep.

10. Comforting music can also be played, and you can tap as you listen to the music.

USING IMAGES FROM NATURE TO HELP WITH SLEEP

Joanne was having difficulty sleeping at night. She found that as soon as she lay down and closed her eyes, her mind would begin to race. Instead of letting go into peaceful slumber, she was making lists of things she had to do.

In order to help calm her mind, she decided to tap in a resource. She imagined a place in nature that made her feel peaceful. It was a high Sierra lake near Tuolumne Meadows in Yosemite National Park. She had backpacked there one summer with her husband. The lake was deep blue and surrounded by craggy granite peaks. The water was so clean and clear that she could see shimmering rainbow trout darting among the rocks on the lake bottom. The mirrorlike surface reflected the mountains and pines. As she imagined the lake she opened her other senses. She could smell the water, the fragrance of trees, sweet-scented wildflowers, and a hint of wood smoke. She could feel the warmth of the sun on her skin and a gentle breeze blowing. She could hear the sound of a distant water-fall and the wind in the trees. She imagined looking out at the scene and how peaceful she felt. When she had the scene filled in as much as she could and felt her body relaxed, she began to tap on the sides of her legs, right-left, right-left. She tapped as she imagined the peaceful scene. When she began to feel sleepy, she stopped tapping and drifted off.

CHAPTER 5

Trauma First Aid

Turn your face to the sun and the shadows fall behind you.

—MAORI PROVERB

HARRIET WAS DRIVING along a frontage road on a sunny afternoon when out of the blue a car made a left turn right in front of her. As she quickly swerved out of the way, she thought to herself, "Oh no, I'm going to hit the tree!" Then there was a loud crash. The airbags deployed, and smoke filled the car. Fearful that her car was on fire, she quickly opened the door and stumbled out. Safely outside, she scanned her body for injuries. Though she was trembling and her legs felt like rubberbands, she realized with relief that she was all right.

When Harriet got home, her whole body was shaking from the trauma. The scene of the accident played itself over and over in her head. She was stuck in the moment of terror—that *"Oh shit"* moment—and was not connecting to the moment that came soon after when she realized she was okay. She wanted to clear the trauma as soon as possible before she developed post-traumatic stress symptoms such as anxiety, nightmares, or a fear of driving. She lay down on her bed and brought her attention to her body. She then began to tap on the sides of her legs, right-left, right-left, as she recalled getting out of the car and realizing that she was not injured. As she imagined this she repeated to herself, "Nothing's broken. I'm okay." With the imagery and positive statements running through her mind, she tapped until she felt her body take in the information, and she felt herself relax. It took about thirty minutes for the trembling in her body to cease. From time to time over the next day or two, she would tap in the positive image and words, continuing to reinforce them.

After the second day she felt the accident was behind her. Later she found that she was able to drive without it affecting her confidence and sense of safety.

What to Do If You Experience a Trauma

There are several things you can do immediately to help calm yourself in the wake of a trauma, for example, a car accident, robbery, or natural disaster such as an earth-quake, fire, or tornado. The first thing you should do, of course, is to get yourself to safety. Be sure you are physically taken care of. When you are physically safe, remind yourself that you survived and that you are safe now. Then begin to tap bilaterally, right-left, right-left. Tap as long as it feels comforting to you and you feel yourself calming down.

The next step is to integrate the moment of trauma with what happened *the moment after the trauma took place*—the moment that enabled you to survive the ter-rifying experience. Acute trauma often leaves this information unintegrated. We become stuck in the moment of terror, reliving it again and again like a broken record. What we need to do is to lift the needle and place it in the next groove so that we can feel the relief of our survival. The record can then continue to play the rest of the song. By focusing on what hap-pened next and tapping it in, we are able to connect the moment of terror and the moment of survival in our minds. This is what Harriet did repeatedly in the exam-ple above—she reminded herself of the moment when she got out of the car and was okay.

You can also help yourself feel safe by using calming or comforting imagery. Imagining your safe/peaceful place, your sacred place, your nurturing or protector figures, those you love, and spiritual figures can help. Sometimes tapping without imagery is sufficient to

relax your nervous system. Following are several suggestions for using tapping after a traumatic incident.
Please remember that if the trauma feels too big for you
to deal with on your own, seek out an EMDR therapist
who can help you process the experience.

If you have recently experienced a trauma, here are
some of your resources you can tap in that can help:

- You can tap on your knees bilaterally or do the
  butterfly hug to help calm yourself. You can do this
  without any imagery. Tap as long as it feels calming
  to you. You might say to yourself calming words
  such as "I'm okay. I survived." Repeat the words
  and tap. This is much like comforting a baby by
  rocking. The tapping can calm your whole system.

- Imagine yourself after the moment of shock
  and fear. Focus on what happened next. Tap
  as you imagine that next moment of doing
  something, of discovering that you had survived.

- You can imagine going to your safe/peaceful
  place or sacred place. When you feel yourself
  there, begin to tap. Tap as long as it feels good.

- You can imagine your nurturing figures or your
  circle of love (Chapter 13). Feel yourself being
  cared for by these figures. Imagine them with

you in your safe/peaceful place. When you can sense this, tap. Tap as long as it feels good.

- If spiritual figures calm you, you can tap them in.

- If you feel compelled to talk about what happened, do so—but tap on your knees as you talk. In this way you will be processing what you experienced and help it to move out of your system. If you should begin to think of anything else from your life that is disturbing, stop tapping and think of your safe/peaceful place. Then imagine going there while you tap.

- If you need more help, find an EMDR therapist in your area.

USING RESOURCES TO DEAL WITH AN ACCIDENTAL INJURY

One Sunday afternoon Alison was playing tennis with a friend when she had a freak accident. She had hit the ball out of the court and over the fence. A passerby threw the ball back into the court, but wildly. Without thinking, Alison ran to catch it and ran smack into the net pole, impaling her left thigh on a protruding metal hook.

She was aware of the impact, and then blackness enveloped her. The next thing she knew she was on the ground. She looked down at her leg and saw that her black pants were all wet. Her first thought was, "Oh damn, blood. This is bad." She didn't know it then, but she was in shock. People were asking her if she was okay, did they need to call an ambulance, but she couldn't answer. She didn't have a voice. "Where is all this liquid coming from?" she thought to herself. She pulled down her pants to see her leg and found a two-inch long by one-inch wide gash exposing the bone. Trapped in a twilight zone experience, she found she could not do or say anything.

She was transported to an emergency room that was full of sick and injured people waiting to be helped. Soon after her arrival, attendants stabilized her wound with a pressure bandage and left her to wait for a doctor. Because her tennis partner had gone home, she waited for hours alone. Frightened, injured, in shock, and by herself, she realized that she needed to calm herself down. She remembered the resource tapping technique. Crossing her arms in front of her chest, she began to alternately tap each shoulder using the butterfly hug. As she tapped, she repeated to herself, "I'm okay. I'm okay. I'm waiting to be seen. They will come get me. I'm okay." She tapped on and off throughout the long wait. The tapping helped her make it through.

Five hours later, Alison was finally taken to an examining room. On the other side of the room, behind a curtain, she could hear a woman being supported by a group of people. It was then that she realized that she needed someone there with her, too. Usually a confident, independent woman, she understood that she was now completely unable to advocate for herself. But, frozen with shock, she couldn't connect the thought with action. She continued to feel as if she were in an echo chamber with an invisible wall separating her from the rest of the world. Because she was unable to express her thoughts, she had not called anyone to be with her during this time. It is common for traumatized people to be unable to speak, as the part of the brain that controls speech shuts down during a trauma. This is most likely what was happening to Alison. Though she realized she needed help, she couldn't make a phone call. The part of her brain that knew she needed help and the part that controlled her body's actions were disconnected. In order to help her brain make the connection, she began to tap the positive thoughts, "I can call someone. I can call someone and pick up the phone. It is okay to do it, and someone would want to help me." After tapping Alison discovered that she was able to pick up the phone and dial a friend's number. But she still couldn't speak. "At first I just cried into the phone. After she kept asking me questions, I was finally able to tell her where I was and that I needed help."

After the call Alison used tapping to soothe herself again. "Good job. She's on her way. She will get here." These words gave her hope as she continued to wait for a doctor. Soon her friend arrived and was able to talk to the doctor as well as provide support and calm. By the time Alison left the hospital, it was 1:30 in the morning. She had spent eight hours there.

Alison found the tapping to be very helpful right after the injury, during the wait in the emergency room, and also for helping in recovery from the injury itself. I will describe Alison's use of resource tapping to help her heal in Chapter 7.

Helping Someone Else Who Has Been Traumatized

Mark was a young man in his late teens who was man-handled by overly aggressive police officers. Mark was at his girlfriend's house, and they were having a quar-rel. Mark was not threatening her or being violent, but he wouldn't leave when she demanded he do so. She was so angry she called the police. When the police arrived they threw Mark against the patrol car, pulled his arms behind his back, and handcuffed him. They slammed his head against the car. When Mark asked why they were doing this, they threatened to hurt him more. Mark was angered and confused by the aggression displayed by the officers, as he had not resisted arrest. When he cried in pain because the handcuffs were too tight, they refused to loosen them. He was in terrible pain and frightened that the cuffs were cutting off the circulation to his hands.

When Mark was released to his parents, he was hysterical. The police had terrified him as well as physically abused him. He was bruised, and his wrists had red welts around them where the cuffs had cut into them. He was so upset he couldn't stop talking and shaking. He couldn't get over the way he had been so disrespected as a human being and that the officers had had the power to do anything they wanted to him with impunity.

In order to help him, his mother told him to keep talking about what had happened while she tapped on his knees. Mark talked and cried for several minutes while she gently tapped. Every once in a while she would remind him that it was over, that he had survived. Finally he felt done. He was no longer shaking. He felt calmer. They made a plan to write a letter of complaint to the chief of police regarding the officers' conduct.

If a loved one or someone you know has had a recent trauma you can use the following approach.

✳ Tapping In Resources in Cases of Trauma

1. Bring the person to a place that is safe and comfortable. Try to calm the person by talking. Put your arms around the person or even wrap him or her in a blanket. Help the person to feel safe in the present.

2. If it is appropriate, and it is all right with the person, tap on his or her knees, shoulders, or back, right-left, right-left, to calm the person. The person can

also tap on himself or herself. Repeat calming words if it seems to help: "You're okay. You are safe now."

3. Lead the person through guided imagery to a safe/peaceful place. When he or she can imagine the safe/peaceful place, tap a little to help the person feel it more fully. Tap as long as it feels good and safe. Be careful not to let it go into associations of unsafety.

4. If it feels right, have the person imagine nurturing figures or protectors in the safe/peaceful place. The person can tap as he or she feels that, too.

5. The person can imagine spiritual figures and tap them in if that feels right to him or her.

6. If the person feels compelled to talk about what happened, tap as he or she talks. The tapping helps to process the disturbance out of the person's system. Keep the focus on the recent trauma. If the person begins to associate to other incidents, bring him or her back to what recently happened or to the safe/peaceful place. Let the person talk about the whole thing, from beginning to end. It is especially important to focus on the fact of the person's survival and that he or she is safe now. Continue to tap through the entire narrative.

7. Have the person recall what happened after the most frightening part of the incident. Gently instruct the person to focus on what happened next. As the person does this, tap. In this way the person is connecting the moment of terror with the moment of action and fact of survival.

8. If it is appropriate, the person can imagine what he or she would like to do next. As the person imagines it, tap.

9. If the person needs more help, seek out an EMDR therapist in your area.

USING TAPPING AFTER A SKI ACCIDENT

Janet helped her friend Melissa with tapping immediately after a ski accident. They were skiing down a steep slope when Melissa hit a patch of ice and careened out of control. She landed hard, her right shoulder taking the full impact of the fall. When Janet reached her, Melissa was in terrible pain and crying. It looked as if her shoulder was badly broken. Janet wanted to help her friend in some way while they waited for the ski patrol. Because she knew the tapping technique, Janet began to gently tap on either side of the midline of Melissa's back, right-left, right-left, while repeating to her in a calm voice, "You're going to be okay. You're going to be okay. The ski patrol is on the way." As soon as Janet tapped, Melissa began to calm down. She began to talk, finding words to express her feelings, which before were trapped inside her. When the rescuers arrived Melissa was able to describe her needs so that they were able to help her.

CHAPTER 6

Preparing for and Handling Medical and Dental Procedures

Every patient carries her or his own doctor inside.

—ALBERT SCHWEITZER

IF YOU ARE FACING stressful medical situations, resource tapping can be a valuable tool. It can be used to help you prepare for a medical or dental procedure, to reduce your stress while you are undergoing treatment, to aid in recovery from medical procedures, and to promote healing.

In this chapter I will show you how you can use resource tapping to help you with stressful medical situations.

Preparing for and Coping with Medical and Dental Procedures

Do you dread going to the doctor or dentist? Most of us don't look forward to these visits, but some of us experience greater fear, especially if we are dealing with serious illnesses. Activating positive emotions produces immediate stress reduction important for healing. Two of my colleagues in Germany, Christa Diegelmann and Margarete Isserman, specialize in working with people who have chronic illness, particularly cancer patients. They have found resource tapping to be very helpful for their clients throughout the course of diagnosis, treatment, surgery, aftercare, and also palliative care. Resource-focused work can help alleviate our distress immediately, and also help enhance coping, decision-making, and general functioning.

There are many ways you can make use of imagery to help you through a medical or dental appointment or procedure. Abby, who was receiving radiation for breast cancer, imagined the radiation as healing light from the universe coming down through the crown of her head into the area of cancer, bringing healing. As she imagined this she tapped on her legs. While Chloe received her chemotherapy, she tapped as she imagined her inner helpers there with her as supports and visualized the chemo as healing water running through her system, curing her cancer. As Marge sat in the dentist chair she tapped on her knees and imagined her special place in the meadow and was able to feel calm throughout the procedure. Many of my clients, friends, and colleagues have tapped in resources to cope with medical procedures and have found it very helpful. In some cases, along with the decrease in anxiety, it has even significantly decreased the experience of pain.

Whether you are dealing with a minor but anxiety-producing medical procedure or facing a serious illness, resource tapping can help you feel more at ease and in control.

You can use tapping in a variety of ways leading up to, during, and after a medical or dental procedure.

Before the procedure

You can help decrease anxiety about an upcoming medical procedure by tapping in resources at home. You might tap in healing imagery or imagery that you find calming or comforting.

Before an appointment with your doctor

You can tap in resources prior to speaking with a physician to help you think clearly and be better able to ask your questions and express your concerns. After initially calming your system by tapping in resources, you might rehearse what you want to say to your doctor and then tap as you imagine it. For example, you might want to imagine feeling calm and confident as you ask your doctor about the anesthesia, pain medication, details of the procedure, and expected recovery time.

In the waiting room
You can tap in resources as you wait in the waiting room to calm yourself down. Close your eyes and go inside. Bring up your resources and tap. You can discretely tap your fingers on the sides of your legs without anyone noticing. You can even tap your toes in your shoes.

During the procedure
You can tap in resources during the procedure itself.

After the procedure
You can tap in resources after the procedure is over. You can tap in images of healing, comforting, safety, whatever feels best to you. You can also tap in the fact that you survived, you are okay, you got through it, it is over, you will heal now, and so on. This gives your body the signal that it is no longer under attack and can relax and recover.

Which resources you should tap in depends on which ones would be most comforting in the situation. Ask yourself what it is that you find most distressing about the situation and what would help you feel better. Do you need safety, comfort, protection, or spiritual guidance? Resources that you may find useful include the four basic tools (safe/peaceful place, nurturing figures, protector figures, and inner wisdom figures, all covered in Chapter 3), comfort resources including the circle of love (see Chapters 12 and 13), calm and peaceful resources (see Chapter 14), uplifting resources (see Chapter 16), spiritual resources (see Chapter 17). You can look at the Appendix for more ideas. Healing imagery can be used with tapping before, during and after the procedure.

USING RESOURCES TO GET THROUGH
A DENTAL PROCEDURE

Connie dreaded going to the dentist. She always felt very anxious. She hated going so much that she put it off until her teeth were so bad that she needed a lot of work done. Having learned about resource tapping, she was determined to use this tool in the dentist's office and have a better experience.

As she sat in the chair, white bib around her neck, waiting for the dentist to begin giving her the painful shots, she closed her eyes and entered a peaceful inner space. She remembered her sacred place (see Chapter 17) high in the mountains, with its majestic peaks and crystal clear lake. When she could feel the place strongly, she began to tap her knees. She tapped until she felt her body release, a sigh escaping from her lips. She then imagined her spiritual figures—her angel with broad, welcoming wings and Jesus emanating love. When she could imagine and feel these figures, she tapped. She tapped until she felt them strengthen inside her.

Now when the dentist asked her to open her mouth so that he could inject Novocaine, she felt relaxed. As the needle went in, she tapped her knees again, imagining her sacred place and spiritual figures. She noticed, as she tapped, that the shot didn't hurt very much. She felt comfortable. She stopped tapping and rested for a few minutes before the dentist began his work. Then, when the drilling began, she imagined herself in the arms of her angel, with Jesus by her side, and resumed tapping.

The time in the dentist's office sped by. She felt comfortable and relaxed the entire time. She felt in control. She could do it. The dentist was relieved that Connie felt so much better, especially since she had more visits before the work would be finished.

USING THE CIRCLE OF LOVE RESOURCE TO PREPARE FOR A MEDICAL PROCEDURE

I recently had the opportunity to tap in resources to help me cope with a medical procedure myself. My doctor advised me to take antianxiety medication prior to the procedure. When I asked him why, he told me that the procedure was uncomfortable and caused many people to feel anxious. I opted to use meditation and imagination with tapping instead of the medication.

While I waited in the exam room for the procedure, I closed my eyes and went inside. I then brought up images of my favorite place, a place on a beach where I love to walk and swim. As I imagined myself there, I tapped on my knees to strengthen the image. I then imagined people who love me and whom I love. I brought each one to mind, and when I could see them clearly and could feel their love, I tapped on my knees. I repeated this process with each of my loving resources. Then I imagined myself in the middle of a circle with my loving resources surrounding me, a visualization I call the "Circle of Love." Focusing on each loving person, one at a time, I imagined a ray of warm, loving golden light coming directly from each person into my heart center. I took each one in until I felt love light coming from multiple sources. It was like I was the center of a wheel with light from around the circle flowing into me. My heart felt warm and full of love. I felt protected, cared for. When I had the image and feeling of love strong inside me, I began to tap on my knees again. I continued for a few minutes, letting the feelings strengthen. As I tapped I found myself releasing deep sighs of relief. I felt my body relax. I even had tears run down my cheeks as I felt the love and caring of my resource people. Then I began to direct my love light back to my loving resources. I gazed at each of them in turn, feeling my heart radiating love back to each one. I imagined golden light flowing from my heart into their hearts. I felt an uninterrupted stream of warm, enlivening energy. I continued with the imagination and tapping until the nurse came to get me for the procedure. I felt wonderful! My heart was warm and expanded; I was peaceful, relaxed, and completely at ease. I was able to maintain the feeling during the entire procedure, which took about an hour. I was so relaxed the doctor even remarked on it to the nurse. (See Chapter 13 for more on the Circle of Love resource.)

CHAPTER 7

Healing Illness
and Injury

What lies behind us and what lies before us are
tiny matters compared to what lies within us.

—RALPH WALDO EMERSON

IN ADDITION TO using our resources to help us prepare for medical or dental procedures, we can tap in resources to help us heal from illness and injury. Research has shown that imagery can aid in healing, and as such it has become part of treatment for many diseases. One of the most well-known researchers in this area, O. Carl Simonton, describes in his book *Getting Well Again* how patients' use of healing imagery can arrest and even reverse the progress of cancer by boosting the functioning of the immune system. We can augment the power of imagery by combining it with tapping.

By using resources we've already tapped in (safe/ peaceful place, nurturing figures, protector figures, inner wisdom figures) as well as others that we feel will help us, such as healing imagery, positive memories of health and wholeness, and encouraging words, with tapping we can elicit our body's healing capabilities. To illustrate many of the resource tapping tools that can be used to help in healing, we will return to the story of Alison, whom you read about in Chapter 5.

Alison is an EMDR therapist who was already familiar with resource tapping when she accidentally impaled her left thigh on a hook while playing tennis, gouging a hole that required sixteen stitches to close. Beyond traumatizing Alison physically and emotionally, the injury also affected her ability to operate her leg; the muscles in her leg were not working at all. She learned from her doctor that the blunt force trauma she had experienced had erased her brain's programming for the use of those muscles. Though no nerves were severed, her brain could no longer tell her leg to move. Her doctor told her that the brain could relearn to operate the muscles by repatterning through physical therapy. But even with this reassurance that her leg would eventually heal, Alison was terrified that she would never walk again.

In order to counter her despair and to give herself hope, Alison decided to apply her understanding of the principles of resource tapping to her current problem. In the process she also discovered an innovative and effective way to use tapping for retraining her leg and aiding the healing of her injury.

The first thing Alison thought to do was to focus on her doctor's encouraging words and tap on each shoulder, right-left, right-left. While she tapped she would repeat to herself, "This will heal. This will heal." On and off during the days following the injury, she would tap for several minutes repeating these positive words. She found that, indeed, the tapping helped give her hope and decrease her fear.

Though the tapping helped alleviate much of the emotional upset, by the seventh day postaccident, despite her work in physical therapy, she still could not move her injured leg. She learned exercises in physical therapy but found that she was not able to do them on her own. Her leg would not respond to her commands.

Then she had an idea. Maybe if she helped her injured leg *remember* what it felt like when it was healthy, it would begin to find the pathways to movement. Each time she was not able to lift her leg off the bed and felt fear, she took the following steps. First, she focused on her doctor's positive, reassuring words—"you can heal this"—and tapped to strengthen the feeling of hope. She would feel less fearful immediately. Next, she called upon her higher power or wise self, which also told her, "You can deal with this," and tapped. This also served to increase her sense of hope and to decrease her fear. Then she imagined herself being active—running, skiing, and playing tennis—and tapped in those images. She went on to imagine all of these resources together—the doctor's encouraging words, her inner wisdom figure's supportive words, and the memories and images of her being physically active—and tap. Finally, she linked the positive words and positive body memories with images of herself doing the physical therapy exercise, and tapped. In this way she transferred the feeling of hope and the healthy leg memories to her injured leg.

After tapping the resources, she tried the physical therapy exercise again. She was delighted to discover that her experiment worked! Whereas prior to the resource tapping she had not been able to lift her leg at all, now she was able to lift it off the mattress a little bit.

After this initial approach, Alison discovered another way to enhance her progress in physical therapy. She called upon her good leg to teach her injured leg how to move again. She would begin by moving her good leg, paying close attention to the sensory experience of the muscles being used. As she slowly, mindfully moved the leg, she tapped on her shoulders, helping her body to remember and take in more fully what it felt like when all the muscles were working. Then she moved her attention to her injured leg. She recalled everything she had learned with the good leg, all the sensory information she had collected. She invited her bad leg to imitate the experience of her good leg. Transferring the memory of the healthy leg onto the injured one, she tapped more.

After she did this, she would try to move the injured leg again. She saw an improvement. She did several rounds of tapping in the healthy leg's sensory experience and transferring it to the injured leg, going back and forth from one leg to the other. Each time she did this she noticed that her injured leg was better able to move.

Over the days that followed, she tapped in her resources and practiced her exercises. Her physical therapist was impressed with her progress, which far exceeded what had been anticipated. Alison was able to successfully retrain her muscles at a faster rate than she would have accomplished without the resource tapping. Tapping in memories helped her body remember the pathway to wholeness.

In order to harness your body's healing memory, you want to activate memories of health and wholeness and then transfer them to the area that is unhealthy or injured. Think of it like merging two files or covering the dark with light; the healthy part infuses the unhealthy part with healing. It seems that when our bodies remember what it feels like to be healthy, their healing is facilitated.

✳ Tapping In Health to an Unhealthy or Injured Part of Your Body

1. Bring your attention to the part of your body that is unhealthy or injured. Notice what it feels like. Is there a color, shape, or temperature associated with it?

2. Now bring your awareness to a part of your body that feels healthy. Notice what it feels like. Is there a color, shape, or temperature associated with it?

3. If you can't locate a healthy feeling in your body, recall a time when your body was healthy. What were you doing? What did it feel like?

4. When you have a strong sense of the healthiness, tap. Tap right-left, right-left, 6 to 12 times. If the good feeling is getting stronger and feels positive, you may tap longer if you wish.

5. Now invite the healthy image, sensations, or temperature to transfer over to the unhealthy part of your body. You can imagine the healthy part transposing onto the unhealthy part, mixing with it, or suffusing it with vibrancy. You can use an image such as white light to represent the feeling of health and allow it to fill the unhealthy part. As you imagine this, tap 6 to 12 times or as long as it continues to feel positive.

6. You can go back and forth between the sense of the healthy and the unhealthy part, repeating the steps as much as you like.

7. Imagine yourself healthy and whole in the future. Tap as you imagine this.

More Suggestions for Tapping In Resources for Healing

There can no longer be any doubt that our health is deeply impacted by our thoughts and feelings. Guided imagery alone has been shown to aid in healing and speed recovery time. Because resource tapping is such an effective way to harness the power of imagination, it can be especially potent when applied to health issues. Here are a few more ways to utilize resource tapping for your health.

- You can tap memories of times when you healed in the past. For example, if you had an injury and got better, tap the memory of how you healed. Remember that your body knows how to heal itself. If you had an illness, remember that you got better.

- To inspire hope, you can tap in the image of someone you know or have heard about who recovered from an illness or injury. Bring up an image or memory that represents this person's healing and tap.

- You can tap in healing imagery. What images do you associate with healing? What image would help your body to heal? What does your body need? As you imagine it, tap. One woman who received chemotherapy for her cancer treatment felt her body had been poisoned. She imagined herself under a beautiful waterfall, the cleansing water purifying the toxins from her body. As she imagined this healing imagery, she tapped on her knees.

- Imagine yourself healthy and whole. Tap as you imagine this. Remind your body that it can heal itself.

CHAPTER 8

Overcoming Problems

Although the world is very full of suffering,
it is also full of the overcoming of it.

—HELEN KELLER

IF YOU HAVE a current life difficulty or are facing challenges in your life, you can use your inner resources to
help you. These challenges might include difficulties
in your relationships or work. You can apply this technique to dealing with your boss, asking someone for a
date, coping with your in-laws, or finding the strength to
help an ailing loved one. In this chapter I will provide a
step-by-step guide to finding and tapping in resources
that can help you handle a current problem. You can read
and follow the steps on your own, or if it works better for
you, ask a friend or family member to guide you through

them. Following this, I provide you with additional ideas for overcoming obstacles. Again, if you have an extensive trauma history, it is always advisable to get one-on-one help from an EMDR therapist.

✳ Tapping In Resources for a Current Life Difficulty

1. Think about the current situation that is difficult for you. What is challenging you right now? When you think of this situation, what image or scene comes to mind?

2. As you think about this situation, ask yourself what quality or qualities you need to better deal with it. What resource or resources might you need?

3. Now ask yourself when you have had that quality or qualities.

4. Next, bring the image or memory of the resource you have chosen to mind in more detail. What do you see, hear, feel, smell, or taste? What emotions do you feel? What do you feel in your body?

5. Focus on the resource and the positive feelings, and begin to tap. Tap 6 to 12 times initially, right-left, right-left. Stop and check in to see how you feel. If the positive feelings have gotten stronger, continue for two to three more rounds of tapping. Stop tapping when you feel that the resource has been strengthened. If the resource has become negative, stop immediately, and consider choosing another resource.

6. If you cannot think of a time when you had the quality you need, you can think of someone else who has the quality or qualities. It could be someone you know personally, someone from a movie, TV, or book, a historical or religious figure, or anyone else. It could even be a symbolic representation of this resource or an animal. Review the resources you have tapped in before (safe/peaceful place, nurturing figures, protector figures, inner wisdom figures, or positive memories). One of them might be helpful to you now.

7. Now return to the scene or image that you began with that represented your current situation, difficulty, or challenge. What do you notice?

8. If you feel good, the resource integrated, you can tap to strengthen it.

9. If you need to bring more qualities or resources to the situation, you can repeat the steps for as many different qualities that you want to develop and strengthen.

10. You can imagine using your resources in the future in different situations, tapping as you do this.

USING RESOURCES TO OVERCOME A WORK PROBLEM

Jane was having difficulty at work. She felt intimidated by one of her coworkers, an older woman who was very critical of her. Whenever this woman approached Jane's desk, Jane became speechless, felt incompetent, and could hardly think. Jane was puzzled by her reaction because this woman was not in a position of authority over her. Nonetheless, this was a pattern she had experienced in relationship to many women.

When her therapist asked her why she thought she reacted to her coworker in this way, Jane said she had difficulty feeling her own power and standing up for herself. Her therapist then asked her what picture came to mind that was most upsetting to her when she thought of the situation with her coworker. Jane said that when the woman came up to her desk and looked down at her, she saw the furrow in the woman's brow and heard the edge to her voice. When she imagined this scene, she noticed that she felt afraid.

Her therapist then asked Jane what quality or qualities she would need to handle the imagined scene the way she would like. The words "strength" and " power" came to her. Her therapist then asked her if she could think of a time when she had those qualities, a time when she felt strong and powerful. Jane closed her eyes and went inside herself, searching her memory for a time when she felt strong and powerful. After a few minutes she came up with a time when she was running a 10k race and felt very strong.

Jane's therapist instructed her to evoke this memory as fully as she could, paying special attention to how she felt in her body. When she had a well-established feeling of strength and power, she should begin to tap on her knees for 6 to 12 times or longer, as long as it continued to strengthen and feel positive.

Jane tapped for a short time and found the feelings strengthening, particularly the feeling in her arms and legs. She continued tapping, letting the sensations more fully assimilate into her whole system. As she tapped, she remembered other times when she was strong.

When the positive associations finished, her therapist directed her to return to the image of her coworker, asking what she noticed now when she thought of it. Bringing up the picture of her coworker and checking in with her own feelings, Jane noticed that she felt bigger, stronger. Her therapist told her to tap some more, tapping in these good feelings with the image of her coworker. Finally, she asked Jane to imagine returning to work the next day and her coworker coming up to her desk. This time Jane felt strong and powerful. Her therapist then instructed her to imagine and feel that as she tapped. Jane tapped as she imagined this future image. When she was done, she said she felt ready to see how it worked.

What if Jane had been unable to think of a time when she had felt strong and powerful? Sometimes we just can't think of an example from our own experience. If that should happen, you can look for someone or something else that possesses the desired qualities. In Jane's case, she could search for someone or something that had the qualities of strength and power. She could have come up with an image of a mountain lion, imagining the mountain lion exhibiting strength and power. When she felt those qualities, she could tap to strengthen and integrate them in herself. Then, when she imagined the scene with the coworker, she would bring the qualities tapped in from the mountain lion into the scene.

More Suggestions for Tapping In Resources to Overcome Problems

Sometimes life brings us challenges we don't believe we have the strength to handle. We can feel demoralized and weak, doubting our capacity to carry on. We can strengthen and tap in memories of having overcome problems, or use examples of others who have done so. By recalling and tapping in these resources, we can see that we have it within ourselves to do what we need to do.

* ### Tapping In Memories of Overcoming Problems

1. Close your eyes and go inside. Bring your attention to your inner experience. Focus inward. Now bring to mind a time when you were able to overcome a problem. Think of a time when you were able to triumph over something difficult for you.

2. When you find the memory, find a scene that most represents the feeling of overcoming the problem.

3. When you bring up the image, what are you seeing? What do you hear? What are you feeling in your body?

4. When you have a strong sense of overcoming the problem, tap 6 to 12 times. Stop, and see how you feel. If it is getting stronger, tap longer.

5. You might ask yourself, "What did I learn from this experience?" When the answer comes to you, tap it in to strengthen and integrate it.

6. If you would like, think of another time you were able to overcome something difficult for you.

7. When that memory is strongly evoked, tap it in.

8. What did you learn from that experience? Tap to integrate that information.

9. Now bring to mind a situation from your current life that is difficult for you, a situation that requires this information you have tapped in about overcoming difficulties. When you think of it now, bring the information you have learned from the past to this experience. When you have a positive feeling of it, tap. Tap as long as it feels good.

10. You can tap as you imagine yourself in the future using the information you have received.

USING MEMORIES TO OVERCOME AN OVERWHELMING FAMILY PROBLEM

Nancy had an ailing mother who was losing her ability to function independently. She felt so overwhelmed by all the things she had to do to help her mother that she couldn't move forward. The obstacles seemed endless. Furthermore, she couldn't find the strength within herself to overcome these problems.

She took a few moments to go inside, to locate the quietness inside herself. From this place she recalled times in her life when she had been able to overcome difficulties, times in her life when, despite the problems, she had prevailed. She recalled a time when she was facing a medical issue. She had had to do research, consult different physicians, and talk to friends and family in order to resolve what had seemed so difficult at the time.

As she recalled that experience, she contacted that part of herself that was able to persevere through it all. When she could feel it in her body, she began to tap. She tapped 6 to 12 times, strengthening the memory and taking it into her system. What did she learn from that experience? She learned that she could handle only one day at a time and not to project into the future. Projecting into the future was a waste of precious time and energy. She also learned that when things are difficult, you need the loving support of others.

As she reflected on what she learned, she tapped to integrate this information. When that felt complete, she thought of another time she was able to overcome difficulties. She strengthened and integrated this memory, too, by tapping. She also reflected upon and tapped what she had learned from that experience.

After tapping in these memories, she returned to her current situation with her mother. She checked in on how she felt. She noticed that she felt better able to handle the situation. She tapped to strengthen and integrate this information. She tapped lessons learned from the past that she could apply to the current situation, saying to herself, "I can handle one thing at a time. I can focus on each task that is before me. I can ask for help."

Finally, she tapped on her knees as she imagined herself in the future applying what she had learned. She imagined herself calling her best friend for support, finding a therapist, and contacting a support group.

ROLE MODELS

We can draw from the stories of other people overcoming difficulties in their lives to encourage us. Who has inspired you? There are many inspiring books and stories about people overcoming great difficulties and life challenges—from well-known celebrities like Lance Armstrong, Michael J. Fox, and Sidney Poitier, to ordinary people you may have heard or read about. Characters from movies and works of fiction and mythology can also be used as resources.

✳ Tapping In Examples of Other People Overcoming Difficulties

1. Close your eyes and go inside. Take a few moments to calm yourself and arrive at the present moment. Now think of someone who has overcome difficulties. Who has persevered through difficult situations? It can be someone you know, someone you have heard or read about, or a character from a movie or a book.

2. When you have the image or memory of the person exhibiting this quality, notice what he or she looks like. What expression is on his or her face? What is he or she doing?

3. As you imagine this person, notice how you feel. What sensations do you experience in your body? Can you feel the strength and determination the person displays?

4. When you can feel this determination, begin to tap. Tap 6 to 12 times. If the quality is getting stronger, tap longer. Feel the quality in yourself. As you recognize it in this other person, realize that it is also within you.

5. Is there someone else you would like to imagine who has overcome obstacles? Bring this person up too, and when you have a strong sense of him or her, tap to strengthen the feeling.

6. Think of your current situation in which you are facing something difficult.

7. Bring in the resource person you have tapped in. Feel the quality he or she would express. Feel the quality as it would manifest in you. For example, if you tapped in Nelson Mandela's determination, perseverance, and courage, feel those qualities in yourself. Evoke Nelson

Mandela as you face your difficulties; bring his qualities that are also your own into action in your life. Tap as you feel this applied to your current situation.

CHAPTER 9

Boosting Performance

Energy is the essence of life. Every day you decide how you're going to use it by knowing what you want and what it takes to reach that goal, and by maintaining focus.

—OPRAH WINFREY

RESOURCE TAPPING WORKS well for enhancing performance. It can be used for sports, public speaking, acting, writing, and test taking. In this chapter I will provide you with many tools you can use to help boost your performance. We'll start with a basic step-by-step guide for performance enhancement. After this I will give you more tools and ideas, which can be used alone or in combination.

If you are trying to boost performance in a particular area, you may begin by imagining yourself doing whatever the activity is. Then ask yourself what qualities or resources you would need to be more successful. Bring to mind memories, experiences, or representations of the resource you need. After you have done this, activate the resource as strongly as you can, with all of the sensory information that accompanies it, and then tap it in to strengthen it. After the first resource, you might want to add more. When you feel you have all of the resources you need, imagine bringing these resources to the current situation. For example, if you have tapped in the resources of memories of a piano recital during which you played well, memories of feeling confident, apply those tapped-in feelings to imagining playing the piano in the future. In this way you are linking the stored information networks of playing the piano well and feeling competent with the imagined future situation.

 ## Tapping In Resources to Boost Performance

1. Bring up an image of doing whatever you are planning to do. For example, if you are anxious about making a speech, you might envision a future scene with you standing in front of a large audience.

2. Ask yourself what resource or quality you need in this situation. For example, you might say that you want to be a confident speaker.

3. Think of a time when you had the resource. Can you think of a time when you were a confident speaker? If you can, bring an image or memory to mind that represents that time.

4. With the resource in mind, activate your senses. What do you notice in your body? What are you feeling? For example, you might remember a time when you felt confident giving a speech that went well. You bring up the memory of giving that speech. You see yourself standing in front of the audience, feel the strength in your legs, hear your voice, strong and confident. Bring in any other senses that will help fill in the details. When you have a good sense of the resource, begin to tap. Tap 6 to 12 times. Stop and check in to see how you are feeling. If the resource continues to strengthen, tap some more.

5. Are there encouraging or coaching words that go with the positive image or memory? There might even be music that inspires you (the theme song to *Chariots of Fire,* for example). Tap the memory or image with the words or music.

6. If you can't think of a time when you had the resource, you can think of someone else who has the resource. It can be someone you know, or someone you have read or heard about. If you are thinking about giving a powerful speech, for example, you might think of someone like Maya Angelou.

7. Elicit the image and feelings associated with the resource as strongly as you can. In our example, you would bring up an image of Maya Angelou speaking. When you imagine her, notice how you feel. Can you feel the sense of confidence she emanates?

8. You can tap in a cue word if you like. Once you've activated the resource, say a word to yourself that is associated with the resource. In our example, you might say "Maya" and tap to link together the word and resource.

9. After tapping in the resource, return to the image you began with of the future performance. For example, imagine giving the speech—what comes up for you now?

10. If you feel better, more confident, tap to strengthen these feelings. Tap as you imagine giving the speech, feeling your resource inside you.

11. If you feel the need for more resources, tap them in, too.

12. Finally, imagine yourself in the future, performing with your resources inside you. Imagine giving your speech from beginning to end feeling confident. Tap as you imagine this.

USING PERFORMANCE-BOOSTING RESOURCES FOR A SPORTING EVENT

Hanna was nervous in anticipation of a one-hundred-mile bicycle race she was riding the next day. Even though she knew that she'd be picked up by a truck if she became too tired and needed to stop, she still felt anxious. She decided to try resource tapping to help her.

First, she wanted to address her anxiety and feel more relaxed. She decided to tap in a safe/peaceful place. She loved to go to the beach, particularly a certain beach in Mexico. She imagined her beach, bringing in her senses—what she saw, smelled, felt, and heard—as much as possible. When she could feel herself there and could relax, she tapped on her knees, right-left, right-left, like she was drumming. She tapped for a few minutes. Soon her shoulders dropped, she let out a soft sigh, and she felt more relaxed.

Hanna also wanted to contact her confidence in riding. To do this, she tried to recall a time when she felt strong and competent riding her bicycle, a time when her legs were powerful and she could really ride well. She thought of a time and tapped on her knees right-left, right-left, as she imagined that time, paying special attention to her body. It felt good. She then thought of words she could tell herself as she rode, things like "I can do it," and "I've got the power." She said the words to herself as she remembered her ride and tapped her knees.

She then recalled other memories of riding well and tapped as she replayed them in her mind. Finally, she thought of Lance Armstrong, who was inspiring to her. She brought up an image of Lance riding and tapped that in. She felt great.

Finally, she wanted to bring all of the resources she had tapped into her imagined ride the next day. She visualized the entire ride going successfully, feeling the power and confidence her resources provided her. She also told herself, "I can do it." She tapped on her knees for several minutes, going over the entire imagined course. When she finished, she opened her eyes and said out loud with a smile, "I know I can do it. If I need to I can stop. I'm going to have a great time no matter what." And she did!

More Suggestions for Tapping In Performance-Enhancement Resources

Along with the guide to performance enhancement I outlined earlier, there are several other things you can do. The following resources can be tapped in to help boost your performance:

- Inner mentor or coach

- Inner support team

- Memories of success

- Imagining your goals actualized

- Strengthening successes

You can read through this section and develop the best plan for your particular situation. Find the resources that work best for you. For many people a combination is most helpful. In order to decrease anxiety, for example, you might tap in your safe/peaceful place first. Then you might boost your self-esteem and self-confidence by tapping in an inner coach and an inner support team, as well as including memories of being successful. After that, you can imagine yourself performing at your peak and tap that in. To keep yourself motivated, you can tap in the image of achieving your goal on a regular basis. If you are a runner, you can imagine the race course and running through all the parts of the course successfully, all the way to the end. If you are planning to speak in front of an audience, you can visualize speaking successfully, full of confidence.

INNER MENTOR OR COACH

The inner mentor or coach is a resource that can be imagined and tapped in to provide you with specific help in an area of need. It can be used for the enhancement of performance and even for help with habits and addictions. The inner mentor can be someone you know personally such as your life coach, fitness trainer, therapist, clergyperson, or someone you have read or heard about. The inner mentor can also be a part of yourself.

✳ Tapping In the Inner Mentor or Coach

1. Close your eyes and go inside. Take some deep breaths, and slowly let them out. Relax, and let go with each exhalation. Spend all the time you need to quiet your mind.

2. When you feel yourself present, imagine your safe/ peaceful place. Imagine yourself in this special place where you feel relaxed and at ease. Take the time you need to really feel the serenity and peace of this place. When you can feel it, begin to tap. Tap right-left, right-left, 6 to 12 times. If you want to tap longer to strengthen the feeling, you can do so.

3. Now bring to mind someone real or imagined whose support and encouragement would be of value to you. Accept whatever image comes up for you. It can be someone you know, someone from a movie or a book, or someone you have heard about elsewhere.

4. When you have an image of your inner coach or mentor, notice how you feel in your body. If the feelings are positive, tap right-left, right-left, 6 to 12 times to strengthen it. If you want you can tap longer.

5. Does your coach or mentor have a name? If you like, you can give your coach a name and tap as you imagine him or her, the feelings associated with him or her, and his or her name.

6. Now imagine your inner coach or mentor giving you the advice and support you need at this time. You may hear words, get a feeling, see an image, or receive the information in some other way. Just notice what comes to you.

7. When you receive the message or advice, begin to tap. Tap as long as it feels positive.

8. Imagine taking the advice your coach has given you. What would your life look like? When you have a strong image or feeling of this future, tap. Tap as you imagine taking your coach or mentor's advice. Tap as long as it strengthens in a positive way and feels good.

9. Remember that you can contact your inner coach or mentor whenever you need his or her advice or support. Just bring your coach to mind, say his or her name, and tap. In this way your coach will always be available to you.

INNER SUPPORT TEAM

Along with your inner coach or mentor you can also tap in an inner support team. These can include helpers, role models, friends and family, and even imaginary figures. Maybe there was a coach, personal trainer, or supportive friend you had in the past who can become a resource now. Your nurturing figures, protector figures, and inner wisdom figures may be included on this team. Who would you like to have on your support team?

✳ Tapping In Your Inner Support Team

1. Bring to mind someone you would like on your inner support team. It can be a friend, family member, partner, coach, or role model—someone you know personally or someone you have seen or read about. It can be one of your nurturing, protector, or inner wisdom figures.

2. As you bring this person to mind, feel his or her support for you.

3. When you can feel the support you get from him or her, begin to tap.

4. Tap 6 to 12 times, and then stop and check in to see how you are feeling. If the positive feeling for your resource person is getting stronger, you can tap longer.

5. Tap in as many supports as you would like. With each one you can feel the sense of support increasing.

6. Imagine yourself surrounded by your support team. You are in the center of a circle of support. Spend a moment and look at each one of your support people. Feel their support for you. Take it in; feel it as strongly as you can in your body.

7. Tap as you look at and take in the support from each one of your team members.

8. Now feel the combined support from your entire team. When you can strongly feel the sense of support in your body, begin to tap. Tap as long as it feels positive.

9. Imagine taking this feeling of support with you into your life. When you have an image or sense of doing this, tap to strengthen it.

10. Remember that your support team is always there. All you have to do is think of them and tap.

MEMORIES OF SUCCESS

If you are having difficulty motivating yourself because you are focusing too much on feelings of inadequacy, you can counteract these feelings by strengthening memories of times in the past when you were successful. For example, let's say you have to take an exam and are feeling anxious and insecure about your ability to do a good job. You can bring to mind a time when you did well and felt confident taking an exam and then tap as you imagine it. When you do this, it is important to activate the sense experience as much as possible. It is especially important to focus on the body feeling of performing well. In this case you would see yourself taking the test, see the exam in front of you, feel yourself sitting, focusing on the sensation in your body. Emphasize the feeling of power and success, the feeling of your thoughts flowing easily. Once you have a strong positive sense of the experience, begin to tap. Tap as long as the resource continues to be positive. Imagine yourself taking a test in the future. Tap as you imagine this.

Tapping in success can also be applied to sports. You can bring up memories of doing well at your sport, times of being in "the zone." If you are playing tennis, you might bring up a time when you were playing very well. You would bring to mind what you were seeing, hearing, and smelling, and the sensations in your body as you hit the ball. You can even stand and place your body in a position that will enable your body to better recall the experience. You want to activate as fully as possible the positive athletic experience. When you have done this, tap 6 to 12 times, then stop and check in with how you are feeling. If it continues to be positive, you can tap longer. After you have done this, imagine yourself in the future, taking this body-based confidence with you. Tap as you imagine this.

✳ Tapping In Memories of Success

1. Close your eyes and go inside. Take some deep breaths, and slowly let them out. Let yourself relax, and let go with each exhalation. Spend the time you need to quiet your mind.

2. Think of the activity or sport you would like to be more successful at.

3. Bring up a time when you were successful at the activity or sport. Think of a time when you were in "the zone," you were in a flow, you felt good about your performance.

4. When you bring up that experience, notice what you see. Look around you. What are you hearing? What are you feeling in your body? You might want to stand or place your body in a position that will help it recall the experience more fully.

5. When you have a strong sense of the experience, tap. Tap right-left, right-left, 6 to 12 times. If the feeling is getting stronger, you can tap longer. Tap as long as it feels completely positive.

6. If you would like, you can bring up another time you were successful at your activity. Tap it in the same way.

7. Now imagine yourself in the future being successful in your activity. Take the body-memory sense you have tapped in to the future situation. When you

can feel it strongly, tap to strengthen and integrate the experience.

IMAGINING YOUR GOALS ACTUALIZED

Many athletes make use of the imagination to help them achieve peak performance in their sport. By visualizing themselves performing at their best, and evoking the feeling in their bodies of being in "the zone," golfers, baseball players, tennis players, ice skaters, runners, and others can increase their performance. These same principles can be applied to many areas of performance, including test taking, public speaking, acting, and even managing problem behaviors such as overeating or drinking.

You can imagine accomplishing your goals and then tap that in. Imagine playing the perfect game of tennis or golf, or skiing effortlessly down the mountain. If you wish to be successful at taking a test, imagine doing your best with confidence, and tap that in. You can reinforce whatever your goals are by regularly imagining your goals actualized and tapping to strengthen them.

✳ Tapping In the Image of Your Actualized Goals

1. Close your eyes and go inside. Take some deep breaths, and slowly let them out. Relax with each exhalation. Feel yourself coming to the present moment. Take as much time as you need to quiet your mind.

2. Think of a goal you have in your life right now. You might be preparing for a bike ride, a tennis match, a public speech, a music recital, or an exam of some kind.

3. Now imagine yourself accomplishing your goal. Fill in details with your imagination as much as you can. See and feel yourself doing it. When the image feels strong and well-activated, tap to strengthen the feeling. Continue to tap as long as it feels positive.

4. What other goals do you have? You can help in the development of your goals by writing them down. You can imagine and tap in a positive future with these goals also.

STRENGTHENING SUCCESSES

We all know that praise is a better motivator than punishment, yet most of us do the opposite with ourselves. Rather than acknowledging and celebrating our successes, we spend too much time in life focusing on what we have done wrong, what we have left to do, or what we could have done better. We spin in the negative circuitry of our minds, feeling perpetually inadequate. But we can train our minds to do something different.

By activating and tapping in experiences of success, we can strengthen and integrate them. Whether they're large or small, through tapping in our successes we can raise our self-esteem and bring a more balanced perspective to our lives. If it helps, we can practice a positive life review on a regular basis. At the end of the day we can review what went well. What were we successful at? As we review the successes, and can feel them in a positive way in our bodies, we can tap them in.

If you have set goals for yourself, it is helpful to review what you accomplished and then tap to strengthen and integrate the information. Take the time to specifically recognize and absorb into your system what you got done. Hold the positive image, body sensations, emotions, and any positive self-statements, such as "I did it," while you tap. In my therapy work I have devoted entire sessions to tapping in successes so that clients could more fully take them in.

TAPPING IN THE DAY'S ACCOMPLISHMENTS

Adrian worked a demanding yet enjoyable job at a law firm. He cared deeply about the work he was doing but felt he often made commitments he could not keep, due to his heavy workload and a drive to be all-accomplishing. He would put off simple tasks he had said he would do out of his feeling of overwhelm. Missed deadlines and unanswered queries resulted in angry clients and frustrated coworkers. So Adrian set a personal goal for himself of meeting every commitment he made: he called it "100 percent follow-through." His goal was both to follow through on things he promised to do and also to turn down work when necessary so as not take on more than he could realistically handle.

Each evening before going to sleep, Adrian would review the day's work and recall each follow-through he had accomplished. He used the butterfly hug and tapped in the feeling of relief and satisfaction that arose with each faxed document, emailed reply and completed task. He tapped in the feeling of strength and confidence that came from saying "no" when his workload had reached its limit. He tapped while thinking, "I really helped that person today," and "My boss knows she can count on me." Back in the office he found it easy to use tapping to access the resource of his previous successes any time he felt the famil-iar resistance to the tasks at hand, thus helping him to reach his goal.

CHAPTER 10

Opening Creativity

*A work of art always arises from the background:
consciousness. Be it music, painting, architecture,
poetry or sculpture, it is always seen by the
artist in an instant, like a flash of lightning,
as it surges forth from deep within him.*

—JEAN KLEIN

WHEN WE ARE creative we are in touch with deep aspects of ourselves, and we express them in form. We feel connected to ourselves and to our lives. Often we find ourselves in a flow, outside of time, where the "me" disappears in the process, and there is just creating. When we are low and depressed, it can be difficult to find the energy to be creative. Yet when we begin to express ourselves, even a little, we discover that the act of creating will itself lift our spirits. If you feel blocked in your creative expression, you can use your resources to help you.

✳ Tapping In Creativity

1. Close your eyes and go inside. Spend a few moments quieting your mind. You might imagine going to your safe/peaceful place or your sacred place (see Chapter 17).

2. Imagine expressing yourself creatively in whatever form you wish. Now ask yourself, "What is preventing me from expressing myself? What beliefs, feelings, or memories are in the way?" For example, let's say you want to write. You imagine yourself trying to write. You see yourself sitting at your desk in front of your computer, and you can't think of anything. The belief that arises is, "I can't do it. I can't make a mistake." You feel fearful and insecure.

3. After you have imagined this, ask yourself what quality or resource you would need to help with this. Listen to what comes up for you. In our example, you want to feel confident. Think of a time when you had this resource, a time when you persevered despite feeling afraid. If you can't think of a time when you were confident in your creativity, think of another time when you felt confident. It doesn't have to be a creative example.

4. With the resource in mind, activate your senses. What do you notice in your body? What are you feeling? For example, you might remember a time when you were playing baseball. You were up at bat. You felt anxious, afraid of blowing it, but you stepped up to

the plate, focused, and hit the ball well. Bring up the memory and see yourself standing at the plate. Feel the bat in your hands. Feel yourself hitting the ball and running hard. Bring in any other senses, and fill in the visual details. When you have a good sense of the resource, begin to tap. Tap 6 to 12 times. Stop and check in to see how you are feeling. If the resource continues to strengthen, tap some more.

5. Ask yourself if there are any encouraging or coaching words or music that go with the positive image or memory. If so, tap the memory or image with the words or music. Even just thinking "I can do it!" will work.

6. If you can't think of a time when you had the resource, think of someone else who has it. Elicit the image and feelings associated with the resource as strongly as you can. You might think of Georgia O'Keefe, a painter with exceptional strength and courage. You imagine Georgia O'Keefe, feeling her qualities of strength and courage, and tap.

7. You can tap in a cue word if you would like. Once you've activated the resource, say a word to yourself that is associated with the resource.

8. After tapping in the resource, return to the image of creating you began with. For example, imagine writing—what comes up for you now?

9. If you feel better, more confident, tap to strengthen these feelings. Tap as you imagine writing, feeling your resources inside you.

10. If you feel the need for more resources, tap them in, too. For example, you might want to feel more playful. You imagine two otters frolicking in the water. The imagery makes you feel happy, looser. You tap in this imagery and the feelings it evokes. Finally, imagine yourself in the future, creating with your resources inside you. Imagine writing from beginning to end, feeling good all the way. Tap as you imagine this.

More Suggestions for Opening Creativity

You can use the following other resources individually or combine them in any way that feels best to you:

- If your creativity is blocked because of anxiety, you might want to use resources to decrease your anxiety (see Chapter 4). Tapping in your safe/ peaceful place or sacred place (see Chapters 3 and 17) are good ways to begin. This helps to clear your mind and bring you to the present moment.

- Try tapping in resources of love (see Chapter 13). Because our inner critics often close us down, activating and tapping in resources of love can open us to compassion and our creativity. Begin with your safe/peaceful place, and then proceed with one or more of the love resources. After completing this, turn your attention to your creative project.

- You might want to tap in spiritual resources to help inspire you (see Chapter 17), or tap in your inner wisdom figure and ask it for advice (see Chapter 3).

- Tap in someone else who is creatively open. Use him or her for inspiration. You can also tap in an inner mentor (see Chapter 9).

- Focus on resources that are uplifting and that can help pull you out of a feeling of contraction (see Chapter 16).

- If you had a friend who was creatively blocked, what advice would you give him or her? Tap in the advice you give, and then imagine taking it.

- Tap in a positive future. Imagine expressing yourself creatively. Forget that you feel blocked. Imagine yourself doing what you want to do with as much detail as you can. Tap as you imagine this.

Sometimes just focusing on and tapping in many different memories of being creative can open you up and help get you going. This next practice will help you strengthen this resource.

✳ Tapping In Memories of Being Creative

1. Close your eyes and go inside. Take a few moments to bring yourself to the present. Take some deep breaths, and relax as you exhale. When you feel present and relaxed, bring up a time when you were creative, a time when you were immersed in doing something you loved to do. It can be a time when you expressed yourself through music, art, writing, acting, or in other ways. What is important is that at the time you felt good about expressing yourself creatively.

2. When you have the memory, open your senses. What are you seeing? What are you hearing? What do you taste or smell? What sensations do you notice in your body? How do you feel when you are creative?

3. When you have a strong sense of being creative, begin to tap. Tap 6 to 12 times, then stop and check in to see how you are feeling. If you are feeling good, and the feelings are continuing to be positive, you can continue to tap. If other memories of creativity arise, you can tap them in, too.

4. When you feel complete, stop tapping. Now take a few moments and notice how you feel. What do you notice in your body?

5. If you feel inspired to express yourself creatively, take a moment to imagine what you might like to do. If you would like, you can tap as you imagine being creative in the future. (For example, imagine buying canvas and paints, setting the time aside to paint, going to your studio, and then seeing yourself painting.)

USING A MEMORY OF PAINTING
TO REGAIN INSPIRATION

Evelyn was feeling low, stuck in her life. She had little motivation to do anything. Though she was an artist, it had been months since she had even entered her studio to paint. I asked her if she could remember a time when she was creative, a time when she was actively involved in her painting. She told me she could. Several months ago she had been working on a painting she was passionate about. As she spoke of it, she brightened up a little. I decided to help her tap in the memory of painting. I asked her to close her eyes, go inside, and spend a few moments bringing herself to the present. When she indicated to me that she felt present, I asked her to bring up the memory of when she felt very creative, a time when she was immersed in her painting and felt good. I told her to take as much time as she needed to locate the memory. When she told me that she had found it, I asked her to strengthen the senses as much as she could. What was she seeing? What did she smell? What did she hear? What did her body feel like? I asked her to let me know when she could remember the feelings of being creative, the feeling of being in a flow. When she indicated that the memory was strong, I asked her to tap on her knees, right-left, right-left, 6 to 12 times, then stop and tell me what was happening.

Evelyn was silent as she tapped. When she stopped, she told me the feeling was getting stronger and that other memories of painting and being creative were coming up. I told her that she could continue to tap as long as the memories and feelings were positive. After a few minutes she stopped tapping. She had a smile on her face and told me that she felt much better.

I then asked her if she could imagine painting in the future. If so, she could take this good feeling and apply it to an image of the future. She tapped as she imagined herself painting. When she was finished she said she felt inspired to paint for the first time in months.

CHAPTER 11

Supporting Recovery from Addictions and Other Problems

A man can only do what he can do. But if he
does that each day he can sleep at night
and do it again the next day.

—ALBERT SCHWEITZER

MANY OF THE resource tapping techniques used for performance enhancement described in Chapter 9 can be used to help support you in your recovery process from addictions and other destructive habits. Resource tapping along with EMDR is being incorporated into a comprehensive treatment for addictions in many centers throughout the United States. California psychotherapist A. J. Popky has developed an addictions treatment model called DeTUR—Desensitization of Triggers and Urge Reprocessing. (For more information, see his chapter "DeTUR, an Urge Reduction Protocol for

Addictions and Dysfunctional Behaviors" in the book *EMDR Solutions*, edited by Robin Shapiro.) Many of the resource tapping suggestions I have included here are used in this protocol.

Suggestions for Tapping In Resources to Support Recovery

Resource tapping is not a substitute for professional treatment or twelve-step work, but it is a very helpful adjunct to these approaches to addiction recovery. Here are some ways to support your recovery with resource tapping.

- Tap in your four basic resources: safe/peaceful place, nurturing figures, protector figures, and inner wisdom figures. You can imagine them in a circle of support and tap that in. Tap in an inner mentor or inner sponsor to help you.

- In order to reduce anxiety you can tap in resources that bring comfort and peace and calm (see Chapters 12 and 14). Tapping in those you love and who love you, as well as the circle of love, can be helpful (see Chapter 13).

- Empowerment resources can be very helpful. Recall times when you felt resourceful, powerful, and in control. As you activate these memories, be sure to really feel them in your body, and then tap them in. Other empowerment resources (see Chapter 15) include core inner strength, power figures, courage, and memories of saying no and setting boundaries.

- Tap in spiritual resources: spiritual figure, higher power, image of a wise being, essential spiritual self, spiritual experiences, spiritual teachings, insights and life lessons, and loving-kindness meditation (see Chapters 13 and 17).

- Tap in uplifting resources (see Chapter 16) such as gratitude, favorite things, experiences of awe and wonder, beauty, joy, humor and laughter, inspiration, and freedom and expansion.

Suggestions for Handling Urges

Resource tapping is particularly useful when the urge to return to old behaviors threatens your recovery. Here are a number of ways you can use tapping to help maintain self-control.

- When the urge arises to drink or use drugs, overeat, or engage in other addictive or undesirable behaviors, ask yourself, "What resource or resources do I need to help maintain my recovery? What resources would help me control myself?" Listen to what comes to mind. Then think of the resources you have tapped in, or think of some others that might be even more helpful to you. For example, if you feel you need more support, you might choose to tap in your sponsors or friends as supports. You could imagine and tap in your inner support team, circle of inner helpers, your twelve-step group, or other supports. As you do this, take in the feeling of them supporting you in your recovery.

- Memories of health and strength can be tapped in. Can you remember times when you were able to behave in a healthy way? For example, can you remember a time when you were able to stay sober or maintain a healthy weight? If you can, then bring up a positive memory from that time, and tap to strengthen it.

- You can tap in someone you admire who has been a role model for you. Draw inspiration from this person.

- You can imagine your goals actualized and then tap in your positive future. What would your life look like if you attained your goal? For example, if you are trying to lose weight, you might imagine what you would like to look and feel like in the future. In what positive ways would your life change? When you can really imagine it, tap to strengthen and integrate this future projection. You can tap in your actualized goal several times a day, reinforcing in your mind and body this positive future.

- Strengthen successes! Reward yourself by focusing on your successes and tapping them in. For example, if you remained sober for the day and called your sponsor when you were triggered, tap in your success. You might spend time at the end of each day recalling and tapping in your successes.

Resources That Support Weight Loss

If you are in a weight-loss program, such as Weight Watchers or Overeaters Anonymous, and you want support, here is what it might look like to use resource tapping. If you have been educated about proper nutrition and what you need to lose weight in a healthy way, you can review what you have learned and tap. In this way you are reinforcing and integrating this information. If you are still having difficulty with the program, ask yourself, "What do I need to control my eating?" If there are certain triggers to overeating, imagine what you need to eat in a healthy way. What quality do you need? If it is self-control, can you think of a time when you had self-control? If so, bring up a memory of when you had self-control, and tap to strengthen it. Can you think of someone you know who has self-control? You can tap that person in as an inspiration and support, or you can tap in a coach or mentor. Tap in all of the resources you would need in order to fulfill your goal. After you have tapped in these resources, return to the triggering situation. See how you feel. If you need more resources, tap them in. Imagine yourself using your resources in the future when you are triggered.

Many people overeat because they are feeling anxious. Perhaps what you need are resources to decrease your anxiety. You can imagine and tap in your safe/peaceful place and your nurturing, protective, and inner wisdom figures. See Chapter 4 for ideas for managing anxiety, or review the complete list of resources in the Appendix for more ideas.

Weight loss can take a long time and that can be discouraging. Tapping in your successes on a regular basis is important to keep you motivated. Reinforce your success by tapping any and all successes you have during the day. Times when you made healthy choices even while anxious or triggered can be tapped in. For example, if you took a walk instead of raiding the refrigerator, tap that in along with words of praise: "Great job. You did it."

On a regular basis, tap in your goals for the future. What do you want to look like, feel like? What do you want your life to look like when you reach your goal weight? Imagine shopping and buying clothes you like. Imagine hiking and feeling healthy and strong. Tap as you imagine your goals. Tell yourself as you tap, "I can do it."

✳ A Healthy You

PERHAPS YOU WOULD LIKE TO LOSE WEIGHT, EXERCISE MORE, AND LIVE A HEALTHIER LIFESTYLE, BUT YOU FEEL HELPLESS TO TAKE CONTROL OVER YOUR HEALTH. OLD HABITS CONTINUE TO OPERATE ON THEIR OWN, PREVENTING YOU FROM ACHIEVING YOUR GOAL. IF SO, HAVE SOMEONE READ YOU THE FOLLOWING SCRIPT, OR RECORD IT FOR YOURSELF.

Close your eyes and go inside. Take a deep breath in, filling your belly, chest and throat, hold it a moment, then exhale slowly, from your throat, your chest and your belly. Relax, let go with the exhalation. Now take another breath, take your breath in from deep in the earth, filling your belly, chest, and throat. Hold it a few moments . . . now exhale releasing from your throat . . . chest . . . and belly. Relax, let go. Let yourself settle into the present moment.

Now, imagine what your life would be like if you ate a delicious, healthy diet, exercised regularly, and attained your ideal weight. Let yourself enter a reverie. See yourself as you would like to be, living the way you would like to live, and feeling healthy and vital. How would you spend your time? What enjoyable activities might you engage in? What would you wear? How would you look? How would you feel about yourself? Take as long as you like filling in the details of your experience.

When you have a strong sense of this positive future, tap. Tap as long as it feels positive. You may even notice that the path toward your goal begins to reveal itself. Know that when old habits assert themselves you can access this sense of your energized and healthy future self any time by simply tapping.

Part Three

MORE RESOURCES & RESOURCE IDEAS

CHAPTER 12

Resources for Comfort

In the sweetness of friendship let there be laughter,
and sharing of pleasures. For in the dew of little
things the heart finds its morning and is refreshed.

—KAHLIL GIBRAN

IN CHAPTER 3 I described the most easily accessed comfort resource: a safe/peaceful place. In this chapter I will provide you with a number of other resource ideas that you can tap in to elicit the feeling of comfort. You can use these resources when you are feeling anxious, or depressed, or when you simply want to calm yourself. The chapter begins with an alternative to a safe/peaceful place called a "body safe place," and then describes how you can tap in comfort memories and food memories as resources to soothe you. Finally, you will learn how you can combine music, chants, prayers, and lullabies with tapping.

Creating a Safe Place
in Your Body

Another method for finding a safe place is to locate a place in your body that feels safe, a place that is free from any disturbance or conflict. This is a body safe place. Your body safe place is a part of your body that feels uncontaminated by trauma or pain. It can be a place where you feel relative expansion or openness. Even a neutral place, such as your elbow, can suffice. Once you've tapped in a body safe place, you can return there when you are feeling distressed and want to rest.

✳ Tapping In Your Body Safe Place

1. Close your eyes and go inside. Spend a few moments quieting your mind and settling your body. Take some deep breaths in, and then slowly let them out. Relax with each exhalation. Let the stress melt from your body.

2. When you feel relaxed and present, see if you can find a place in your body where you feel a sense of safety. Spend a few moments inside yourself, scanning for a place in your body that is slightly more comfortable than the rest of you.

3. When you identify the place, bring your attention there, and begin to tap. Tap 6 to 12 times, then stop. See how you are feeling. If you would like to tap longer, you can. Tap only as long as it feels positive.

Comforting Memories

You can also use memories of comfort as resources. These memories can include anything that evokes a feeling of comfort and well-being. They can be memories from childhood or adulthood, as long as they evoke completely positive feelings. Memories of cooking a delicious meal, being held by your grandmother as she rocked you in her large rocking chair, baking cookies with your children, holding your cat on your lap and gently stroking his fur as he purrs, snuggling in bed with your partner, having a heartfelt, connecting conversation with a close friend, and listening to or playing a favorite piece of music can all be used as comfort resources. You don't have to be passive in these comforting memories; they can include times when you were doing something, when you were engaged in an activity that gave you a feeling of well-being.

Compiling a List of Comfort Memories

• Spend a few moments and reflect on times in your life when you felt a sense of comfort and well-being. Look for experiences when you felt present and whole. They can be experiences from your daily life like gardening, petting your dog, or reading a good book and can include experiences from your childhood.

• When you identify a comfort memory, spend
a few moments strengthening it by bringing in
more sensory detail. What are you seeing, hearing,
smelling? How does your body feel? Notice
how you feel inside when you remember the
comfort scene in this way. Are you feeling more
relaxed? It is important to focus on the sensations
in your body. You want to feel free of anxiety.

• Now bring up another comfort memory. Again,
spend time bringing it fully into your memory.
Open up your senses. Notice how you feel when
you do this. Can you see how just thinking about
these times of comfort affects how you feel?

• Write down a list of comfort memories. You can
also draw pictures to strengthen the memories.

Some of my best comfort memories are from the time
I spent with my grandparents at their summer home
on a lake in Wildrose, Wisconsin. These were some of
the happiest times in my childhood. When I think of
Wildrose, I see my grandparents' cottage with the green
shutters that looked out on small, blue Round Lake.
There was a little wooden dock from which we would
fish with my grandfather for bluegill and sunfish. We
would catch them with worms we bought at the little

store in town. After gently removing the hook from the wiggling fish, my grandfather would insist we return it back into the lake. My grandparents made this a loving, comforting place for us. My grandmother cooked delicious meals from the fresh local produce, and my grandfather played with us during the day, taking us swimming, turtle catching, and fishing. At night we would play cards for nickels and dimes. When I bring up these memories I feel loved and comforted. I can see the scenes clearly in my mind. I can smell the lake and feel the humidity on my skin. I can see my grandparents—my plump grandmother with her fleshy arms ready to hold me and my bald-headed grandfather with his big smile and hearty laugh.

✳ Tapping In Comfort Memories

1. Think of a comfort memory from the list you compiled, a time when you felt comforted, a time when you had a sense of well-being.

2. What picture comes to mind when you think of your comfort memory that evokes *completely* positive feelings?

3. Now bring in the senses associated with this memory. What are you seeing? What are you hearing? What are you smelling? What does your body feel?

4. When you have the memory well established, and you have only positive feelings, begin to tap. Tap right-left, right-left, 6 to 12 times. Tap longer, as long as it remains positive.

5. You must be able to hold this image in a consistently positive manner and actually strengthen the image through the sets of tapping. If memories or feelings begin to arise that are not positive, see if you can put the disturbance in a container to close off and contain the unpleasant feelings or memories. If you cannot do this, return to the first step and find another memory and associated image.

6. If you want to, find a cue word that is associated with the memory and image. Repeat the cue word to yourself as you hold the image and tap.

7. If you would like, locate another comfort memory, and repeat this process. Tap in as many comfort memories as you want.

8. You can practice using this technique to manage distressing emotions. For example, you may want to bring up the comforting images and cue words before going to sleep, giving the speech, and so on, and tap to elicit the positive feelings associated with them.

In the previous example, I use the image of my grandparents at their cottage on the lake. I bring in all the senses associated with the scene, and when I feel relaxed and have a sense of comfort and well-being, I begin to tap on my knees. As I tap I feel the scene more fully. I take in the love that was there for me then and continues to be there for me in the present. If I begin to feel sad, remembering that my grandparents are no longer with me, I stop tapping. I imagine a strong box with a tight lid into which I gently put the sad feelings. I close the box and put the lid on. I return to the image at Wildrose. When I can feel the comfort feelings again, I resume tapping. With the tapping, my body relaxes even more, and my heart softens. I choose "Wildrose" as my cue word. Now repeating to myself "Wildrose," I continue to tap on my knees as I imagine the scene at my grandparents' cottage. I know that if I feel anxious or distressed about something, I can bring up the image of my grandparents' cottage, say to myself "Wildrose," and tap on my knees to bring a feeling of comfort.

Food Memories

You can use memories of wonderful meals you have enjoyed as comfort resource memories to tap in. Thinking of food we have enjoyed brings a sense of pleasure and relaxation. Use your imagination. Open your senses. My friend and colleague Christa Diegelmann in Germany finds that this resource helps bring comfort to many people she works with.

✳ Tapping In Food Memories

1. Think of one of the best meals you have ever had.

2. Activate your sense memory of the meal. What are you seeing? Where is the meal being served? What does the setting look like? How does the food appear? Notice the colors and textures. What aromas

do you smell? Take your time and really smell them. What are you hearing? Who is with you? Are you engaged in conversation as you eat? How does your body feel as you eat the food? Pay attention to the sensations in your mouth.

3. When you feel comfort and pleasure, begin to tap. Tap 6 to 12 times. If it continues to feel good, you can continue tapping. If it feels complete, stop tapping and savor the experience.

4. If you like, you can think of another wonderful meal and repeat the steps from above.

Music, Chants, Prayers, and Mantras

Are there pieces of music, chants, prayers, or mantras that inspire you, soothe your soul? When you wish to be comforted, what music comes to mind? Is there a lullaby you remember that warms your heart? I am moved to a deep inner state with the Gayatri mantra, the world's oldest known mantra for purification and healing, sung by Deva Premal on her beautiful CD *The Essence* and by the angelic voice of Snatam Kaur on her CD *Grace*. Many people are drawn to the resonance of Gregorian chants or Tibetan singing bowls. The gospel spiritual "Amazing Grace" eases some, while others find spiritual inspiration in pieces of classical music or in a jazz solo.

Are there prayers that appeal to you, that touch your heart? You can recite the prayer and, as you feel the positive feelings it evokes in you, tap to strengthen it. For example, the Serenity Prayer—often used in twelve-step programs—can be recited, felt, and tapped in. Pray for peace, for love, for healing, and tap as you pray.

When you listen to a piece of beautiful music, chant, prayer, or mantra, notice how you feel inside. When you can feel a sense of peace, a beautiful vibration, begin to tap. You can tap for as long as you like, as long as it feels good to you. See if it helps you to take in the special vibration. Let the feeling permeate your whole being. Allow yourself to resonate with this feeling.

USING A LULLABY TO COMFORT A CHILD SELF

Sarah was feeling sad and distressed. She was realizing more and more how little love she had received as a child. In order to give her child self—the part of her that had been deprived—love and tenderness, she imagined herself as a child being held by her grandmother who sang her a lullaby. As she imagined her child self being rocked, she sang the lullaby and alternately tapped each shoulder in the butterfly hug. As she tapped and sang to herself, she could feel love and comfort permeating her whole being. She continued tapping until she felt completely relaxed and at ease.

USING A TIBETAN CHANT FOR DEEP COMFORT

Judy felt a strong affinity with Tibetan Buddhist chanting. She had received teachings and initiations in the past, which had made a strong impact on her life. She had found a CD of Tibetan monks chanting that was very inspiring to her. She wished to take in more fully the special vibration of the chant so that its effects would integrate into her being, enabling her to contact a deep sense of comfort. In order to take in the feeling she experienced from this chanting, she put the CD in her player and began to listen. When she could feel the special vibration and feeling of comfort and ease, she began to tap right-left, right-left, on her knees. She tapped throughout the entire chant. She discovered that it worked! She was able to feel the comfort of the mantras more deeply with the tapping.

CHAPTER 13

Love Resources

The way is not in the sky. The way is in the heart.

—DHAMMAPADA

WE CAN FACE the challenges that life presents us with more ease if we can draw from the reservoir of love in our life. Contained in this wellspring are all the memories of loving and being loved, experiences with cherished family and friends from our past and present life. Even though we may lose contact with it, the love we have received never goes away. It continues to abide in our hearts. When we remember those who have given us this gift, it can sustain us throughout the course of our lives, through all the challenges our lives present us. This reservoir of love can be tapped in so that we are better able to make use of the gift. What follows in this chapter are many ideas you can use for tapping in the resource of love.

Those You Love

One of the easiest ways to tap in love is to think of the people you love. By accessing memories and images of those you love, you can contact your soft, open heart—which can help when you are feeling anxious, unsupported, sad, lonely, or needing an infusion of comfort.

 ### Tapping In Those You Love

1. Take a few moments to go inside and quiet your mind. Find that still place within yourself, and rest there awhile.

2. What people and/or animals from your past and present have you loved? You can go all the way back to your childhood, to parents, grandparents, nannies, friends, teachers, or pets you had. Did you have a pet as a child with whom you felt a special bond? You can focus on those who are alive and special to you now. Think of your children, grandchildren, nieces and nephews, or your dog, cat, or horse. Do you have a close friend you love?

3. If the people or animals are deceased and you feel sad when you think of them, see if you can put these feelings aside and focus only on your love for them. Remember that this love never dies. What

they gave to you continues to be a resource for you throughout your life.

4. You might want to imagine a strong container into which you can put your grief, sadness, or any other painful thoughts or feelings you may have. The container can be a treasure box with a strong lid that you can open when you like. In the meantime, putting these feelings inside will allow you to focus on the good feelings.

5. Now bring up an image of a person or animal you love or have loved in the past. Bring the person or animal to mind as strongly as you can. The image should evoke only positive feelings. For example, you might imagine your daughter as a little girl sitting on your lap as you read her a story. As you bring this image to mind, let yourself feel your love for her. Let the feeling of love fill your heart as much as possible.

6. When you can hold the image and the loving feelings, begin to tap. Tap 6 to 12 times, or longer, provided that the feelings strengthen or remain positive.

7. If it becomes negative in any way—if you find sad memories, regretful feelings, and so on—stop tapping. Bring up the image you began with, and try to find the loving feelings. If you find them, tap again, but only for a short time. If you cannot find the positive feelings, think of another person or animal for whom you have loving feelings, and evoke that image and feelings with tapping again. This time only tap a short while.

8. You can repeat this process with many beings for whom you have loving feelings. Bring each one to mind, feel the feelings of love and affection, then tap to strengthen them.

For example, you might begin with your child, then bring in your spouse, your best friend, and then your dog. Bring up the image of holding and rocking your child in your arms. Tap when you feel the feelings of love. Continue until it feels strong, integrated, and complete. Then bring up an image or memory of loving your spouse. Maybe it was when you were together on vacation walking hand in hand on the beach. When you feel that strongly, tap. Continue until it feels complete, more fully embodied. Next, think of a time when you were close to your best friend. Maybe it was having lunch together at your favorite Thai restaurant, listening to one another, offering support and advice. Tap the image and love for your friend. Finally, imagine your loyal dog sitting at your feet gazing adoringly at you as you feel an upwelling of affection for him. Tap that in, continuing until it feels complete.

Those Who Love You

You can also think about all those who love you and tap in the resource of their love for you. You can think of people or animals from your current life or all the way back to your childhood.

✳ Tapping In Those Who Love You

1. Find a quiet place to be. Close your eyes and go inside. Bring your attention to your breath. Take some deep breaths, and slowly let them out, relaxing and letting go with the exhalations. Do this for a few minutes, until you feel yourself present.

2. Now bring to mind someone who loves you. It can be someone from your life now or someone who has loved you in the past. The person can be alive or deceased. This can include parents, children, grandparents, aunts, uncles, brothers, sisters, friends, teachers, caretakers, counselors, and others. You might bring up a memory of being with that person when he or she was speaking his or her love for you, or you might imagine the person expressing love in some other way, such as holding you or gazing at you with warm, tender eyes.

3. As you imagine your loving resource person, you can increase the memory by activating the senses. What are you seeing, smelling, hearing, feeling? Take in the person's loving presence. Feel it in your body. Remember what it feels like to be loved, to be seen. Focus only on positive imagery and feelings. Put aside any memories or feelings of disappointment or loss.

4. When you have a strong sense of your resource person's love for you, begin to tap on your knees or shoulders using the butterfly hug. Tap six to twelve times, right-left, right-left, strengthening the feeling of being loved. Really let yourself take in the feeling

of being cared for. Let the feeling permeate your cells, bringing warmth and well-being to every part of you. If the feeling keeps getting stronger, you can tap longer.

5. If anything negative comes up while you tap, stop tapping and return again to the positive image. Try to stay with only positive feelings. If you cannot do this, bring up another memory of being loved by the same resource person, or think of another person, and then tap to strengthen that image.

6. After tapping in the first image, bring another loving resource image to mind—a friend, child, partner, or other person. When you have a strong image of being loved by that person, tap it in to strengthen it.

7. Continue bringing up images of loving resource people and tapping as long as you like.

Using a Grandmother as a Loving Resource

My grandmother was a person who I know loved me dearly. Though she was a difficult person with a sharp tongue, critical of herself and others, I know she adored me, and I adored her in return. In my mind and heart, I can set aside the prickliness and focus on the good part of her. There are two images I can tap in that evoke the feeling of being loved by her. One is a photograph taken when I was an infant. In it, my grandmother is holding me in her arms, gazing at me tenderly, her eyes soft, moist with adoration, a gentle smile on her lips. Her look is one of total love. When I bring that image to mind and feel into it, my body relaxes, my heart opens, and I feel at peace. The other image I have of my grandmother is a memory of meeting her and my grandfather at the train station when they came to visit us at Christmastime. Carrying packages wrapped in brown paper that contained delicious cookies she had spent weeks baking for us, she would cry with joy when she saw me. Both of these images evoke feelings of being loved by my grandmother. She is in her loving aspect. When I bring up these images I can strengthen them by tapping on my knees or shoulders. I tap until they feel more fully integrated in my body.

Circle of Love

The circle of love uses the loving resources you have tapped in to give you even more comfort and support. The loving resources are imagined in a circle surrounding you, sending you love. You can use this resource when you are feeling low, alone, and needing support. It can be used prior to a medical procedure, when undertaking a difficult task, or to enhance performance.

✳ Tapping In Your Circle of Love

1. Imagine yourself surrounded by the loving resource people you have tapped in. Look around at these people who love you. Feel the sense of support that being encircled by their love brings.

2. Now focus on each loving person one at a time, and imagine a ray of warm light of the color you associate with love coming directly from each person and entering your heart center. Focus on one person at a time, seeing and feeling his or her love light radiating into your heart center.

3. Open to each one until you are receiving love light emanating from multiple sources, radiating from each of them into your heart center.

4. When you can feel the love, begin to tap, right-left, right-left. Continue tapping as long as the feelings are positive. You are the center of a wheel of love; your resource people and their love light are the spokes. Take in this love light. Let it enter your heart and then permeate and radiate throughout your body until you are filled with the love light.

5. Now bring your attention back to your loving resources. Look at each of them, and feel your love for them, one at a time. Now see and feel your heart radiating love light back to each of them. The love light goes from them to you and you to them as a continuous circuit of blissful energy. Stay with this image and the feelings associated with it as long as you can. Bathe in it. Soak it in. Let it support and nurture you. Continue to tap as long as it feels positive.

6. Realize that this love is in you, always available. Feel the connection to those you love and who love you also. Let this connection support you and bring you comfort when you need it. Remember it is always there. If you would like, you can imagine taking the love and support with you into a future situation. Tap as you imagine it.

The Heart as a Place of Refuge

You can use your heart center as a place of refuge, a kind of safe place. It can serve as a gathering place for your loving resources. You can focus on your heart center and then evoke and tap in each resource, one at a time. You can imagine the resources themselves in your heart, or just the *feeling* of them there. By focusing on your heart center and tapping in loving resources, you are creating a resource that you can return to during times of difficulty.

✳ Tapping In the Heart Refuge

1. Bring your attention to your heart center. Let your heart become soft and warm. Breathe easily, in and out of this center, becoming very relaxed.

2. Imagine your heart as a place of refuge, a sanctuary, a place of safety and repose.

3. Now bring to mind someone you love. As you think of that person, feel the love in your heart. If it feels right to you, you might even imagine holding the person in your heart center. Or you might experience in your heart the feeling of love that person evokes for you.

4. When you have the image and feeling, begin to tap. Tap right-left, right-left, 6 to 12 times. Tap longer only if it strengthens the feeling and remains positive.

5. Now think of someone else you love. Tap as you think of that person. Feel your heart center radiating love and warmth. You might experience a string of positive memories or associations. That is fine. Tap to strengthen the positive feelings.

USING THE HEART CENTER REFUGE TO RELIEVE ANXIETY

Bill was depressed and anxious, overwhelmed by the problems in his life. In order to help ease his stress, we used the heart center refuge. I asked him to bring his attention to his heart center and to breathe in and out of it, letting it become soft and warm. I asked him to imagine his heart center as a refuge. When he nodded his head, indicating that he had done that, I asked him to think of his children, whom I know he dearly loves. As he brought each one to mind, he told me he could feel his heart expand, and he visibly relaxed. When his heart felt warm and soft, his body relaxed with the thoughts of his children, I asked him to tap alternately on each shoulder using the butterfly hug. He spent several minutes doing this. At the end he told me he felt much better, his mood brighter and his anxiety relieved.

Loving-Kindness Meditation

I first learned *Metta,* or loving-kindness meditation, from Sharon Salzberg at a Vipassana meditation retreat she was coteaching with Joseph Goldstein in 1976. I also learned meditations from Lama Yeshe that serve to develop love toward self and others. After practicing and teaching these meditations over the years, I have found them helpful for developing compassion. Over time, I have combined elements from these various meditations and have adapted them according to the needs of different practitioners. Tapping can be added to these meditations to further strengthen and integrate the feeling they generate.

Begin your meditation by sitting quietly and relaxing as you inhale and exhale deeply. This breathing can be followed by guided imagery to your safe/peaceful place or sacred place, putting a protective boundary around yourself and bringing in nurturing or protector figures if needed. The loving-kindness meditation can then be done within the safe/peaceful place or sacred place. You can read this script into a tape recorder and play it back, or have someone read it to you. You can also read it to yourself and try to remember the gist of it, and adapt it as you desire. Be sure to find a quiet, undisturbed place to sit. Disconnect the phone, and make sure that you won't be interrupted during the time of your meditation. You can sit cross-legged on a cushion or in a chair with your feet on the floor. It is important that you are comfortable and are sitting in an upright position. Several variations on this meditation, which can be used according to the needs of the practitioner, are included in this chapter. You can tap continuously throughout the meditation, beginning as soon as you experience positive feelings, or tap intermittently using short sets. You can tap on your knees or cross your arms and tap on each shoulder in the butterfly hug.

✳ Loving-Kindness Meditation with Tapping, Beginning with Yourself

Close your eyes and feel yourself sitting. Be aware of the places of contact—your bottom on the cushion and your feet on the floor. Be aware of your breathing, in and out. Feel the breath in your body. Let yourself relax into the present moment.

Now bring your attention to the area of your heart. Breathe in and out from your heart. Let the breath be gentle and natural. In and out . . . in and out. Feel your heart becoming soft and warm. Mindfully observe your breath until you·are calm and your awareness is focused on the here and now. Now begin to send loving-kindness to yourself, repeating the following and pausing between phrases:

"May I be peaceful . . . may I be happy . . . may I be free from suffering. . . . may I be filled with loving-kindness."

Find the words that work best for you. Let the sound of your voice be gentle, with a cadenced rhythm. Think of a parent gently rocking and soothing a child. The idea is to generate a feeling of warmth and tenderness toward yourself. As you send loving-kindness toward yourself, feel your heart becoming soft, warm, and receptive. When you can feel some warmth in your heart, begin to tap. Tap right-left, right-left. Continue tapping through the meditation as long as the feelings remain positive. If for any reason negative thoughts or feelings arise, stop tapping, and return to generating loving-kindness toward yourself. Begin to tap again when positive feelings return.

Now think of someone you love. As you think of this person, allow your natural good feelings for this person to arise. You might imagine your love as a warm, bright light that is glowing in your heart. Now begin to extend loving-kindness to this person:

"May you be peaceful . . . may you be happy . . . may you be free from suffering . . . may you be liberated."

Use the words that work best for you to send loving thoughts to this person. As you do so, you might imagine light radiating from your heart to your loved one. Imagine this warm, luminous energy filling your loved one's heart with a feeling of well-being and loving-kindness. When you have the positive feelings, tap right-left, right-left. Continue tapping as long as it feels positive.

Now let your love flow out to others you care about. Let it extend to your family and close friends. You might even imagine them sitting near you. Repeat the following, pausing between each phrase:

"May you be peaceful . . . may you be happy . . . may you have ease of being."

Imagine the warm, luminous energy radiating from your heart, touching them and filling their hearts. Tap as you feel and see the love energy going out to others.

Continue to send your loving thoughts and energy out to all the other people around you. This feeling can be expanded to include your community, town, state, country, continent, world, and finally the whole universe. Know that the source of this love is infinite, so as you send it out to others you are continually being replenished.

At the end of the meditation you can imagine sending loving-kindness to all sentient beings in the universe:

"May all beings everywhere be happy, peaceful, and free from suffering."

When the meditation is over, sit for a few minutes longer and take in the feeling of love and expansion in your heart center. If it feels right, continue to tap as it expands. When the meditation is complete, remind yourself that you can always contact this feeling; it is your true nature, your warm, loving heart.

Many people have difficulty beginning this meditation by generating loving-kindness toward themselves. It can be easier to begin by thinking of someone you love or care about, and then turning the love toward yourself.

✳ Loving-Kindness Meditation with Tapping, Beginning with Someone You Love

After relaxing and breathing through your heart center, imagine someone you love in front of you. As you imagine this person, begin to send him or her loving-kindness in this way:

"May you be peaceful . . . may you be happy . . . may you feel joy . . . may you have ease of being . . . may you be free from suffering . . . may you be filled with loving-kindness."

Imagine warm light radiating out from your heart center into the heart of your loved one. When you feel your heart expanding, begin to tap. Tap as long as it continues to feel positive. You might tap a little and then stop, check in with how you are feeling, and then begin again if it still feels good.

"May you be peaceful . . . may you be happy . . . may you know freedom from fear . . . may you feel joyful . . . may you be liberated."

Now, bring up another person toward whom you have loving feelings. As you imagine this person in front of you, begin to send him or her loving-kindness. Tenderly send your loved one loving wishes. When you feel the good feelings, begin to tap. Continue in this way, generating loving thoughts and feelings toward those you love and tapping when the loving feelings are strong.

After you feel your heart expanding, begin to include yourself in your generation of loving-kindness. Repeat the following:

"May I be peaceful . . . may I be happy . . . may I be free from suffering . . . may I be filled with loving-kindness . . . may I have ease of being . . . may I love and receive love . . . may I be free from fear."

When you feel loving-kindness toward yourself, begin to tap. Continue tapping as long as it feels good, the warmth emanating from your heart.

If you wish, you can continue the meditation by expanding the feeling of loving-kindness further as described earlier, to your community, state, country, world, universe, and to all sentient beings everywhere.

The loving-kindness meditation can be adapted to send loving-kindness toward the child self. Perhaps you were abused or neglected as a child, and you find yourself at times reacting more from a child's perspective than that of an adult. You may find yourself frightened, lonely, distressed, or triggered. If you have ever done inner child work or are familiar with your child parts—those aspects of yourself that hold memories from a child's point of view—the loving-kindness meditation can be adapted to help bring comfort to those parts of yourself.

✳ Inner Child Loving-Kindness Meditation with Tapping

Begin by relaxing comfortably. Close your eyes and go inside. Feel yourself sitting, your bottom on the seat, feet on the floor. Take some deep, relaxing breaths. As you exhale, let go and relax. Let go into the earth. Let your body relax, easing into the present moment. Now bring your attention to your heart center. Letting your breath be soft and relaxed, begin to breathe in and out of your loving heart. Imagine your heart as a safe place, a sanctuary. Now imagine your inner child in your heart. Imagine that your loving heart is a safe place for your tender inner child. Begin to send loving-kindness to this child self. In a soft, gentle voice repeat the following, with pauses between phrases:

"May you be peaceful . . . may you be happy. . . . may you be filled with loving-kindness . . . may you be free from fear . . . may you be free from suffering . . . may you be joyful . . . may you feel free . . . may you love and be loved."

Use the words that work for you. Repeat them
silently to yourself as you send loving-kindness to your
child self. When you can feel warm, tender feelings,
begin to tap. If it feels right you can do the butterfly
hug. Tap right-left, right-left. Continue as long as it
feels good. Stop tapping if it does not feel good, and
return to thinking loving thoughts without tapping:

"May you be peaceful . . . may you be happy
. . . may you be free from suffering . . . may
you be free from fear . . . may you be safe."

Continue on in this way, repeating words of loving-
kindness to your child self. You may want to imagine your adult self holding the child in your lap as
you repeat the loving phrases, and other nurturer
resources may also be in the space sending you loving-
kindness. The meditation can focus completely on the
child self, or it can expand to include others. Adapt it
as you see fit.

CHAPTER 14

Resources for Peace and Calm

Peace is our very nature, not something we come across.
It's where we are, nearer than all else.
We don't come to it; we come from it.
To find it is to allow ourselves to go back to the place
we never left.

—DOUGLAS E. HARDING

RESOURCES THAT MAKE us feel peaceful and calm can be developed and tapped in. These resources can be used to help settle us down when we are feeling distressed, to decrease our anxiety, and to serve in quieting us so that we can sleep. We can tap in resources of peace and equanimity by using images from nature, by evoking memories, and by imagining someone else who has these qualities.

Images from Nature

For many of us, nature has provided a refuge and can be a source for positive resource images. Imagining a high mountain lake—its crystal-clear water a mirror reflecting the sky above—can bring a feeling of peace and calm. The vastness of the ocean, in which our problems are seen as mere waves, is another resource image from nature. Imagining a circle of giant redwood trees in a fragrant forest, branches reaching into the sky, roots burrowing deep in the earth, creates the feeling of a peaceful sanctuary. I feel peaceful when I imagine the estuary in front of our Mexican casa near the Sea of Cortez. Great blue herons, egrets, willets, and other shore birds patiently wade in the water hunting for food, their calls punctuating the silence. I also find peace hiking in the Sierras, the trails carpeted with vibrant wildflowers, on my way to snow-fed lakes surrounded by craggy peaks.

SUGGESTIONS FOR DEVELOPING CALM AND PEACEFUL IMAGES FROM NATURE

- Where are your favorite places in nature, places that bring you a sense of peace? These can be places you have been to or places that you imagine. As you think of them, write them down. Make a list with descriptions that elicit your senses. Note what you see, hear, smell, and feel in these places.

- Consider drawing or painting your favorite places. Using art can help you focus on these places and take them in more fully. You

can display your drawing where you will
see it as a reminder of ease of being.

- Take photographs of your peaceful places.
  Exhibit these photos where you can see them.

- Look for postcards of places in nature
  that elicit a feeling of peace and calm.

- Look through magazines, and cut out
  pictures of places you connect with. Make a
  collage by pasting them on a large sheet of
  cardboard. Display it where you can see it.

- If you can, visit these places, and really take
  them in. Open your senses. What do you
  see? What do you hear? What do you smell?
  How does your body feel? You can tap while
  you're there to strengthen the image and
  sensations, so you can easily access them later.
  Actually getting into nature is a wonderful
  way to create a feeling of calm and peace.

* Tapping In Images from Nature That Evoke Peaceful Feelings

1. Close your eyes and go inside. Feel yourself sitting, feel the contact with the seat, your feet on the

floor. Be aware of your breathing. Take some deep, relaxing breaths to settle down. Now bring to mind a place in nature that makes you feel peaceful and calm. It can be a place you've been to or an image from a movie, book, or magazine. You can use any of the resources you developed earlier or something else that comes to mind.

2. Now notice what you see there. Look around. Notice the details of the scene. Pay attention to colors, shapes, and textures.

3. What do you hear? What sounds would you hear if you were there?

4. What do you smell? What do you feel on your skin? What temperature would it be?

5. How does your body feel as you imagine this scene?

6. When you feel a sense of calm and peace, begin to tap. Tap 6 to 12 times, right-left, right-left. Stop and see how you feel. If you feel good and wish to continue tapping, you can do so. Tap as long as it feels positive. If for any reason it feels bad, stop tapping, and either return to the nature resource you began with, or think of another one and begin the steps again.

7. You can add a cue word to your nature resource. For example, if your image is a redwood circle you could say to yourself "redwood circle" as you tap in the image. In this way you can evoke the feeling of calm associated with the image at a time when you need it by saying the cue word and tapping.

8. You can bring up other nature resources and tap them in if you like.

Memories of Feeling Peaceful

We can also use our memories of times when we felt peaceful and calm as resources to tap in. Memories make powerful resources. These memories can include times when you were meditating, praying, doing yoga, reading a book, connecting with a friend, singing with a group, walking your dog, kayaking, swimming, back-packing —anything you can think of that you did that made you feel peaceful and calm.

Spend a few moments thinking of some of these times. Write them down. See how you feel when thinking about them and writing them down. These memories and experiences are in you, accessible when you need them.

✳ Tapping In Memories of Feeling Peaceful

1. Close your eyes and go inside. Spend a few moments bringing yourself into the present moment. Take a few deep breaths, and slowly let them out. When you feel yourself present and more relaxed, bring to mind a time when you felt peaceful and calm—a time when you felt in balance, alive, and whole. It can be a time when you were quiet and still or a time when you were doing something that made you feel peaceful. It can be a recent time or a time long ago. Just let it come to you.

2. Thinking of that time, open your senses. Notice what you see. Look around you. What do you hear? What do you smell? What do you feel on your skin? How does your body feel? Spend some time filling in the sensory details to help enhance the scene and bring it back to you.

3. When you have a feeling of calm, peace, or equanimity, begin to tap. Tap 6 to 12 times, right-left, right-left. Stop and see how you feel. If it feels good, and you would like to, you can tap some more. Continue as long as the feeling remains positive.

4. If you like, you can bring up another memory that feels calm and peaceful and tap that in, too.

Calm and Peaceful Resource Person

Another resource you can use to help you feel peaceful is thinking of someone who is calm and peaceful. Can you think of someone who has these qualities? A person who displays a sense of balance and equanimity? This can be someone you know or someone you have heard about. It can be a character from a movie or book or a historical, religious, or political figure. Examples of people I think of with this quality are His Holiness the Dalai Lama, Mother Mary, the Buddha, Jane Goodall, and Thich Nhat Hanh. It is most important that you *feel* the quality of peace and calm the image of the person evokes.

✳ Tapping In a Calm and Peaceful Resource Person

1. Find a quiet place to sit where you won't be disturbed. Close your eyes and take a deep breath. Slowly let it out. Take another deep breath. As you exhale, let yourself relax and let go, coming to the present moment. When you feel yourself present, bring to mind a person you associate with peace and calm. This can be someone you know or a person from a movie or book. It can be a historical, religious, spiritual, or political person. It can be a real person or someone from your imagination. What is most important is that, when you bring this person to mind, you experience a sense of peace, calm, balance, and equanimity.

2. When you find the resource person, notice what you see. What does the person look like? What expression is on his or her face? Where are the person's hands? Bring in as much visual detail as you can.

3. As you imagine the resource person, notice how you feel. When you feel a sense of peace, calm, and equanimity, begin to tap. Tap 6 to 12 times. Stop tapping and see how you are feeling. If you are feeling good, and the image and good sensations are strengthening, you can tap some more. Tap as long as it feels good and continues to strengthen and integrate.

You can also take your resource person into a present situation you are dealing with that requires the qualities they manifest or represent to you.

Tapping In a Resource Person for Peace and Calm in a Present Situation

1. Think of the situation you are currently in that requires peace, calm, and equanimity. What scene or image comes to your mind when you think of this situation? What is the most disturbing part of it?

2. Bring to mind a memory of your having embodied peace, calm, and equanimity, or imagine one of the resource figures you have tapped in exhibiting these qualities.

3. As you bring to mind the resource, tap 6 to 12 times to activate and strengthen it. Feel the qualities within yourself as you tap.

4. If you would like, bring in another memory of having had the quality or another resource figure. Tap these in as well to further activate and strengthen the qualities.

5. When you have a strong sense of peace, calm, and equanimity, return to the scene or image of your current situation. When you bring it up now, what do you experience?

6. If the scene feels more peaceful than it did earlier, tap a few times to further strengthen and integrate that feeling. If it helps and feels right, you can even imagine your resource figures with you in the scene.

USING PEACEFUL RESOURCES WHEN
CONFRONTED WITH FINANCIAL PROBLEMS

Gary was floundering in debt. His financial problems were troubling him so much that he was ruminating about them day and night and was unable to rest. Fear and anxiety clouded his ability to see the situation clearly.

He found a place to sit quietly and closed his eyes, focusing on his breath. When he was a little relaxed and present, he brought to his mind the picture that represented the worst part of the financial situation. The image that came to him was sitting at his desk and looking at all his bills. This image made him feel anxious and fearful. His mind began to spin, and he noticed his heart rate accelerating. He decided to tap in a resource person who is calm, peaceful, and balanced.

The resource person he chose was the Buddha. He imagined the Buddha sitting quietly, a gentle smile on his face. He was wise and spacious, untroubled by the ups and downs of life. As he imagined the Buddha and felt his peaceful quality, Gary tapped on his knees for a while and felt the sense of peace increase, permeating his whole being. Tranquility, ease of being, and serenity radiated throughout his nervous system. When he felt it well-established, he stopped tapping.

Next, he again brought up the image of sitting at his desk with his bills spread out in front of him. As he imagined this scene, he felt different. He felt peaceful, more spacious. He tapped on his knees a few times to further integrate this feeling into the current situation. He imagined taking this feeling of peace with him into the future as he handled his finances. He tapped as he imagined this positive future. When he completed this exercise, he felt more relaxed and better able to handle his life.

CHAPTER 15

Resources for Empowerment

The sole advantage of power is that you can do more good.

—BALTASAR GRACIAN

EMPOWERMENT RESOURCES ARE resources you can tap in that provide protection, power, strength, and courage. These resources can be used when you wish to summon the strength to face difficulties. They can also help you manage anxiety. You have already been introduced to empowerment resources in Chapter 3—protector figures and the circle of protection. The large selection of resources that follows will provide you with even more tools for empowerment.

Power Resources

Resources that evoke feelings of power in the mind and body can be used to strengthen us, provide resolve, and help overcome obstacles. Power resources include power figures, images from nature, and memories of being powerful.

POWER FIGURES

Power figures are similar to protector figures—you may even use the same ones—but the emphasis is on the feeling of *power* rather than protection. Power figures can include someone you know personally or a historical, religious, political, or sports icon. They can be figures from movies, TV shows, or books. Power figures can be deities such as the Hindu goddess Kali, the giver and taker of life; Vajrapani, the Tibetan Buddhist deity of enlightened power; or a mythological figure such as Zeus or Hercules. It is important that the figure's power be integrated with wisdom and compassion, for unintegrated power can be destructive.

 ### Tapping In Power Figures

1. Close your eyes and go inside. Take a few moments to bring yourself to the present. Find that still place in your being. When you are quieter inside, bring up an image of a figure you associate with power. It can be someone you know or a historical, religious, spiritual, mythological, political, or sports icon. It can be a figure from a movie, TV show, or book.

2. When the image comes to you, bring in more visual details if you can. What does the figure look like? What expression is on his or her face? What posture is he or she in? What is the figure doing? Use these details to evoke the feeling of strength and power as strongly as you can.

3. When you have the image, notice how you feel. Can you feel the sense of power the figure is evoking in you? Where do you feel it in your body?

4. Now, with the image and the feelings of power activated, begin to tap. Tap 6 to 12 times, then check in with yourself. If the feelings of power are getting stronger and continue to be positive, you can tap longer.

5. If you like, you can draw a picture of your power figure.

6. You can also choose a cue word that goes with your figure, and tap it in with the image and feelings of empowerment.

7. Now imagine a situation where you would need to feel powerful. See if you can bring the power resources you have tapped in to the situation. If you can, and if you feel more powerful in the situation, tap to increase the feeling and integrate the resource. Tap as long as it feels positive and you feel strong.

IMAGES FROM NATURE AS POWER RESOURCES

Nature images can also evoke the quality of power. When you think of a hurricane, tornado, tidal wave, earthquake, or glacier, you can use the power of these natural forces. Images of animals exhibiting power can also be used, such as a grizzly bear using its tremendous claws to tear open a honey tree, gigantic blue whales breaching, elephants moving trees, and tigers taking down prey. What nature images do you associate with power?

Remember, the quality of power is not good or bad, but it can be used for good or bad purposes. Please use it with wisdom and compassion.

✳ Tapping In Images from Nature as Power Resources

1. Close your eyes and go inside. Take some deep, relaxing breaths, and slowly exhale. When you feel yourself present, bring up an image from nature that you associate with the resource of power. If you can, identify yourself with that resource.

2. When the image comes to you, notice what you see. What do you hear? How do you feel? What bodily sensations do you notice?

3. When you can feel the resource of power, begin to tap. Tap right-left, right-left, 6 to 12 times. Tap longer if it feels positive, and stop immediately if it becomes negative in any way. In that case, return to the resource you began with, or think of another one.

4. If you like, you can bring up another image of power from nature, and tap it in, too.

5. Tap in as many power resources as you like.

MEMORIES OF BEING POWERFUL

You can tap memories of times when you felt powerful as resources from which you can draw strength. It is important that these memories are of times when you felt powerful and in control. Think of instances when you used your power in a constructive manner, times when your wisdom was also in action.

✳ Tapping In Memories of Being Powerful in a Constructive Way

1. Spend a few moments reviewing your life for times when you felt powerful and your power was used in a constructive manner. These memories must only include times when you did not harm anyone or anything. When did you feel strong and in control?

2. When the memory comes to mind, strengthen it by enhancing visual details and including the senses: what do you see, hear, smell, taste?

3. When the memory is activated and you feel the sense of empowerment, begin to tap. Tap 6 to 12 times, and then stop and check in. If the sense of empowerment is getting stronger, you can tap longer.

4. Bring up another memory of being powerful and effective. Tap it in as well.

5. Tap in as many memories as you like.

USING YOUR POWER RESOURCES

You can use these power resources during times in your life when you are feeling weak and powerless. At these times you can imagine your power resources and tap to activate them, or you can use the following exercise.

✳ Tapping In Your Power Resources When You Feel Powerless

1. Bring to mind the situation where you feel weak and powerless. What image represents it? What are you seeing? Who is involved? What are you feeling?

2. Now bring to mind the image of your power resource. It can be a power figure, an image from nature, or a memory of being powerful. See the resource; feel it. Activate all of your senses associated with it.

3. When you have a strong feeling of your resource, begin to tap. Tap 6 to 12 times. If the sense of empowerment continues to strengthen and feels positive, tap some more.

4. Now return again to the image of your life situation. How do you feel? Can you feel the effect of your tapped-in power resource? If you can, tap again for a short time. This time feel the power you have inside brought to the current situation.

5. If you feel the need, tap in more resources, and then bring them to the current situation.

6. Remember that you have these resources within yourself. You can tap them in whenever you choose.

Core Inner Strength

Core inner strength is the resource that has made it possible for you to face the difficulties your life has presented you. Somehow, you have been able to cope with painful circumstances and have kept going. By tapping in your core inner strength, you can more easily access it as a resource during times of need. Can you think of a time when you were able to persevere despite great difficulties? Can you remember how you were able to accomplish something despite the difficulties?

For example, Dave was able to contact his core inner strength by recalling how, despite lack of emotional or financial support from his alcoholic parents, he had studied hard, gone to a good college, and gotten into one of the best medical schools in the country. He realized that this quality was not dependent on outer circumstances; it resided within him. He could connect with his core inner strength and tap to strengthen it.

✳ Tapping In Your Core Inner Strength

1. Close your eyes and go inside. Now take a deep breath, breathing in from the earth, filling your belly, then chest, and then throat. Hold your breath a moment, and then slowly let it out, exhaling from your throat, then chest, and then belly. Now take another deep breath. Slowly exhale, letting go of all tension. Let yourself relax. Bring yourself to the present moment. Imagine going to your safe/peaceful place. Spend a

few moments in your safe/peaceful place, and tap to strengthen the feeling of peace there.

2. When you feel relaxed, contact your *core inner strength*. This is a part of yourself that has been there since you were born and continues to be with you now, even though at times it may be difficult for you to feel. Your core inner strength is that part of yourself that has allowed you to survive through all the difficult times. Your core inner strength has enabled you to overcome obstacles wherever you have faced them. Take a few moments to get in touch with that part of yourself. Notice what comes up for you. Notice any memories, images, thoughts, or feelings that arise. Notice what you feel in your body as you contact your core inner strength. You may have a memory of when you contacted that part of yourself, or an image may form that represents your core inner strength.

3. When those images, thoughts, feelings, bodily sensations, memories, or images come up for you, and you can feel the sense of your core inner strength, begin to tap. Tap right-left, right-left. Tap as long as the feeling of core inner strength feels positive or deepens in you. If it doesn't feel good, or something negative comes up, stop tapping, and return to memories of feeling your core inner strength or to your safe/peaceful place.

4. You might want to recall and tap in other times when you felt the presence of your core inner strength.

5. When you feel the sense of inner strength well-activated and integrated, remind yourself that in the future, when you wish to get in touch with your inner strength, you will be able to call forth these images, thoughts, feelings, and bodily sensations, and that by so doing you will be in touch with your inner strength again. Continue to tap these thoughts.

6. If you like, imagine yourself in a future situation with your core inner strength. When you can imagine and feel this, tap. Tap as long as it feels good and the positive feelings strengthen.

7. Remember that at any time you want to you can get in touch with your own inner strength by simply closing your eyes for a moment, evoking the images, thoughts, feelings, and bodily sensations, and reminding yourself that you have it within yourself.

Courage

When we are feeling weak and we lack the strength to persevere, we can tap in courage to empower us. We can use memories of times when we demonstrated this quality or use images of others exhibiting it. Feeling courageous does not mean that you don't also feel fear; you may feel fear and courage at the same time. Courage is feeling the fear—and doing what you have to do anyway. With courage we face what is in front of us. We move forward. There is an inner conviction, a strength, we can feel in our legs, arms, and hearts.

MEMORIES OF BEING COURAGEOUS

We can bring to mind times when we exhibited courage and tap to strengthen and integrate them, making the lessons learned from the experiences more available to us. Sometimes we purposely choose to do things that challenge us, and other times life brings us challenges that call forth strength we didn't know we had.

An example from my own life was when I learned to scuba dive. This was something I wanted to do, yet I felt anxious even thinking about it. Somehow I found the courage to take it one step at a time. First I learned to breathe through a regulator underwater. Then I learned how to release the pressure from my ears and to descend safely. I learned how to take my mask off under water and replace it. Next I learned how to handle many emergency situations. Finally, I was able to venture out into the ocean. When I was about to step off the boat into deep water, I was scared to death, but I summoned the courage to do it anyway. And in the end, diving over that coral reef in Belize, I was rewarded with the joy of exploring the extraordinary underwater world.

Now I can recall the feeling of courage that came with learning to scuba dive and can tap to strengthen and integrate it.

✳ Tapping In Memories of Being Courageous

1. Close your eyes and go inside. Spend a few moments in silence quieting your mind. Take some

deep breaths. Exhale slowly, and relax with each exhalation. Once you feel quiet inside, bring to mind a time in your life when you were brave. Recall a time when you were courageous. It can be a moment from your childhood or any time up to the present. It can be a time when you were able to face something difficult or when you defended someone from harm. Just notice what comes to mind.

2. When you locate the memory, find the moment when you felt courage. What did you see? What did you hear? What did you feel inside? What bodily sensations did you have?

3. When you feel the memory activated, and you can feel what it felt like to be courageous, begin to tap. Tap right-left, right-left, 6 to 12 times. Stop and check in with how you are feeling. If the feeling of courage is strengthening, or if you are having other memories of courage, you can tap some more. If it feels complete, stop tapping. If the experience should become negative in any way, stop and bring up another memory of courage or another resource that is helpful to you.

Others as Inspiration for Courage

We can also be inspired by stories of other people exhibiting courage. When we hear of people in difficult situations summoning their inner forces to face challenges, it encourages us to do the same. Inspirational stories may come from movies, TV, books, or from your own family. Have you read or heard stories of courage that have inspired you? These stories can include historical, religious, and political figures, ordinary people who have acted heroically, or characters from fiction. People who inspire courage for many people include Martin Luther King Jr., Joan of Arc, Mahatma Gandhi, Erin Brockovitch, Eleanor Roosevelt, Abraham Lincoln, Jesus Christ, Rosa Parks, Cesar Chavez, Max Schindler, Frederick Douglass, Nelson Mandela, Maya Angelou, Julia Butterfly Hill, and Christopher Reeve.

Some of the narratives that have been inspiring to my clients have come from autobiographies of American slaves, Holocaust survivors, immigrants, and political prisoners. The accounts of bravery presented by these people who lived under such terrible conditions have been a gift for me, providing strength through their example. For one of my clients Frederick Douglass was an important role model. Douglass was born into slavery and endured severe psychological as well as physical abuse yet had the courage to escape and become a great abolitionist and leader. His autobiography, *The Life and Times of Frederick Douglass*, is an inspirational book. There are many great autobiographies of Holocaust victims, which speak to their courage under dire circumstances. A memoir that many people have found particularly inspiring is *And There Was Light* by Jacques Lusseyran, a man blinded in childhood who developed an ability to "see" without physical eyes and worked in the underground during the Nazi occupation of Paris. Lusseyran describes facing capture by Nazis and imprisonment in a concentration camp, as well as the subsequent loss of his closest friends, with clarity, courage, and profound compassion.

Many people have found inspiration in the books *Rain of Gold* and *The Thirteen Senses*, by Victor Villasenor, which cover the history of his family's life in Mexico and immigration to the United States during the Mexican Revolution in the 1920s. His family endured unbelievable hardships yet were guided by his grandmother's spirituality. Other testaments to courage are such books as Nelson Mandela's autobiography, *Long Walk to Freedom*, and Mahatma Gandhi's *An Autobiography: The Story of My Experiments with Truth*. What stories of courage have you read or heard that inspire you?

Developing a List of Inspirational Biographies

1. Spend some time compiling a list of biographies of inspirational figures who have displayed courage, and research their stories. You may read their biographies, watch movies that were made about their lives, or simply look them up on the Internet.

2. In a journal, note what you learned from each one. What scenes were particularly powerful for you? What message was most important?

3. After finishing your research or while you are reading or watching it, tap in the scene or message you want to use in your life.

FAMILY STORIES

We can also draw inspiration from people in our families. Family stories provide us with a personal connection, showing us that even our own ancestors were capable of bravery. Recalling these stories can serve as a resource for us, and we can tap them in to help us find our own bravery inside. Are there stories of courage you have heard in your family? Is there someone you can think of who has demonstrated this quality? Are there stories of acts of bravery that have been passed down through the generations?

FICTIONAL CHARACTERS

We can also find inspiration from fictional characters in literature, movies, or TV. Have you been inspired by a book or movie character who has demonstrated courage? I think of Atticus Finch in *To Kill a Mockingbird*, courageously standing up to the white racists in the courtroom to defend Tom, the black man unjustly accused of raping a white woman, or of Tom Joad from *The Grapes of Wrath*, defending the farm workers.

One of my favorite books is a historical novel by Luis Alberto Urrea called *The Hummingbird's Daughter*. It tells the story of Teresa Urrea, a young Mexican woman who develops spiritual and healing powers after a near-death experience. After word of her ability to heal gets out, thousands of peasants are drawn to her family's hacienda for her touch. Outraged by the atrocities committed by the Catholic Church and tyrannical government officials, she inspires Mexican peasants to rebel. In a dramatic part of the story, she and her father are imprisoned by the government and then put on a train for exile to the United States. The train is full of civilians and soldiers. Not long after leaving the station, she and her father realize that the train has been set up for disaster. Government officials arranged to have the train ambushed and attacked. As the train slowly approaches the canyon where the attack is to take place, Teresa makes her way to the front and stands like Joan of Arc, where all can see her. In a loud, clear voice she orders that no one is to be harmed. No one is to be killed. Though the attackers surround them on all sides, miraculously the train passes through the canyon without a shot being fired.

I can imagine Teresa, a small woman with long, dark hair and kind but penetrating brown eyes, commanding peace from the armed men surrounding her. When

I imagine her, I can feel her courage. When I feel her courage, I can feel it in my own body. I can tap on my knees to strengthen and integrate this experience. When I want to access it, I can think of her and tap.

✳ Tapping In Courageous Figures

1. Take a few moments to reflect on whom you have found to be an example of courage. If you like, you can make a list.

2. Now bring to mind one of your courageous figures. Imagine the person in a situation that evokes the feeling of courage. What are you seeing? What do you feel when you imagine this person?

3. When you have a strong sense of the courageous figure, tap 6 to 12 times, then stop and check how you are feeling. If the feeling of courage is getting stronger and remains positive, you can continue to tap. Tap as long as it feels good.

4. You can bring up and tap in another courageous figure if you like.

5. Think of a situation in which you would need courage. Bring up an image of the situation.

6. Now bring in your courageous figures. Either imagine them to be there with you, or use the feeling of courage they elicit in you to help you face whatever challenge you have. Tap when you can feel courage. Tap as long as it feels positive.

Saying No and Setting Boundaries

There are times when we must be able to say no, to set boundaries with people. It may be difficult to find the strength and self-assurance to say no to someone who is making demands of us. Have you had difficulty setting boundaries with your spouse, partner, children, friends, or employees? You can tap in memories of saying no and setting boundaries. You can also tap in examples of others doing this.

One of the most inspiring stories of setting a boundary I have read is a chapter entitled "Resisting the Slave Breaker" from Frederick Douglass's autobiography, *The Life and Times of Frederick Douglass.* Douglass describes how he has a spiritual revelation that fills him with inner strength and fortitude, after which he knows in his soul that he will never be beaten again. Though he realizes he may be killed if he resists, he will never again allow himself to be degraded by physical abuse. At that time it was illegal for a slave to resist the whip, a deed punishable by execution.

Later that day, when the slave breaker begins to beat him, Douglass grabbs the whip and will not let go. The two men struggle for hours, neither of them willing to give up. The slave breaker's reputation depends on his expertise in destroying men's spirits. He knows that if word gets out that he failed with this slave, his livelihood will be threatened. Douglass perseveres. The man finally gives up and never tells anyone what happened.

After that he leaves Douglass alone, and never beats him again. In fact, Douglass is never beaten by anyone ever again.

✳ Tapping In Memories of Saying No

1. Spend a few minutes reviewing times in the past when you were able to set boundaries and limits. If you like, write them down.

2. Begin with the strongest example you can think of. As you think of it, fill it in with as many visual and sensory details as you can. What was happening? Who was there? What are you feeling as you say no? You want to help your body remember what it feels like to say no, to set a limit.

3. When the image and feelings are strong, tap. Tap as long as it strengthens the feeling and feels positive.

4. If you like, think of another time you said no and were able to set a limit. Access and strengthen that memory by adding sensory information until you can feel the "no," and then tap. Tap as long as it feels positive. If other positive memories of setting limits arise, you can continue tapping.

5. If negative associations arise, stop tapping. Return to the positive memory of saying no, and tap it a few times. You can also go to your safe/peaceful place. Put any unpleasant material in an imaginary container with a strong lid. You can bring in your nurturing figures, protectors, or other allies if you would like them to help you.

If you have difficulty coming up with a time when you were able to say no, you can tap in someone else who has that ability.

✳ Tapping In Others Who Can Say No

1. Think of someone who is good at saying no. You can use someone you know or have known personally, a character from a movie, book, or TV show, or a religious/spiritual figure. The person can be real or imaginary.

2. Bring the person to mind in a situation in which he or she is setting a limit. As you bring the person to mind, what are you seeing? What are you hearing? What do you feel in your body?

3. When you have a strong sense of this person, begin to tap. Tap 6 to 12 times, right-left, right-left. Stop and see how you are feeling. If the feeling is positive, you can tap some more.

4. If you like, you can bring to mind another person who is able to set limits and say no. Tap in that figure as well. You can tap as many figures as you like.

✳ Tapping In Memories of Limit Setting

1. Spend a few moments bringing yourself to the present moment. Take some deep breaths, and slowly let them out. Relax with each exhalation, let go of tension, and settle into the present moment in your body.

2. Think of a time recently when you had difficulty saying no or setting a limit with someone. Bring

the scene to mind as clearly as you can. What are you seeing? Who is there with you? What is happening? What are you feeling?

3. Now bring to mind a time when you were able to say no to someone—a time when you were able to set a limit. Let arise whatever image or memory comes to mind.

4. If you cannot think of a time when you were able to set a limit, can you think of someone else who can? It can be someone you know or even someone from a movie or book. Let the image of that person come up for you. Accept what comes.

5. Once you have the memory or image, evoke the feelings associated with saying no. What do you feel in your body?

6. When the image and feeling of "no" is strongly felt, begin to tap. Tap right-left, right-left, 6 to 12 times. If the feeling of saying no is continuing to strengthen and feels positive, tap some more.

7. Now once again imagine the present situation where you have had difficulty setting a boundary. How do you feel now? Do you feel stronger? If so, tap as you feel your capacity to set a limit in the present situation.

8. If you need more strength, think of another time when you were able to say no, or think of another example of someone else who is good at setting limits. Tap in that example as well.

9. Return again to the scene from the present. How does it feel? If it feels good, and you feel better able to

set a limit, imagine yourself setting a limit with this person in the future. Tap as you imagine it.

Memories of Saying Yes

There are times when we really should say yes but hold back out of fear or habit. We may be in a negative rut we can't find our way out of, or we may be afraid of how others will judge us. If you find this happening to you, one of the things you can do to break this life-limiting habit is to bring to mind memories of when you said yes and tap them in.

 Tapping In Memories of Saying Yes

1. Reflect on a time when you said yes to something and you felt good about it. It can be a time when you took a risk that brought about a positive outcome. It might be a time when you said yes to a new job, a creative project, a friendship, a trip, or a new food.

2. When you can bring up the memory, there should be only positive associations. Now open up your senses. What do you see? What do you hear? What do you feel?

3. When the memory is fully activated, begin to tap. Tap 6 to 12 times, and then check in with how you feel. If you wish, you can tap longer.

4. If the memory should link to unpleasant memories, stop and return to the positive memory you began with. If you can feel the good feelings of saying yes, tap a short time. If you cannot feel good again, go to your safe/peaceful place and rest there. Put anything that is unpleasant in a container with a strong lid. You can bring in your nurturing figures, protectors, or other allies if you wish.

5. You might want to bring in another memory of when you said yes, and tap it in also. When you are done, sit a while and take in more fully what it feels like to say yes. Savor it; know that it is a possibility for you in your life.

CHAPTER 16

Uplifting Resources

*May your walls know joy; may every room hold
laughter and every window open to great possibility.*
—MARYANNE RADMACHER-HERSHEY

THERE ARE TIMES when we find ourselves feeling down, in despair, or feeling that we are lacking something. We can get stuck focusing on what we don't have rather than what we do have. This is particularly true in the United States, where we are constantly bombarded by advertisers telling us that we need to buy what they're selling in order to be fulfilled. What we have is never enough. We are not enough as we are, and we're certainly not loveable as we are. Inevitably, we will become older, fatter, and undesirable. This message undermines our well-being, making us restless and dissatisfied. When we are feeling sad, low, depressed, stuck, and needing a broader perspective and inspiration, we can lift our spirits by tapping in our natural resources.

Gratitude

One way to lift our spirits is to focus on what we appreciate in our lives, what we are grateful for. We can be grateful for many things: the people we love, our health, our work, even the ability to see and appreciate beauty. Even during our darkest times, there are always things we can be grateful for. When we feel thankful, our hearts open, and we are present to ourselves, to others, and to what life brings us. The expression of gratitude is itself a gift, because the openness we feel when we are grateful brings us what we desire most—the feeling of freedom.

Yet there are many unconscious beliefs that keep us from feeling grateful. For many of us, it is easier to focus on what we don't have. Rather than savoring our plenitude, we live in defense against potential loss. You may have an unconscious fear that if you fully appreciate what you have, something bad will happen. You have to be on guard, keep yourself from being vulnerable. You spend your life worrying about the next bad thing that could happen.

You may also fear envy. If you take in the good, really feel how fortunate you are, then someone else will want what you have and try to take it away from you. It's like fearing the "evil eye." Don't compliment my beautiful child, because it will attract something bad that will harm her.

You might also unconsciously fear feeling grateful for your life because it would cause you to become attached to the way things are and make you vulnerable to loss. Nonattachment is a central principle to the practice of Buddhism, but it is often misunderstood. People interpret it to mean that they are not supposed to enjoy their lives. While Buddhism teaches that change is a part of life, many teachers stress the importance of gratitude. There are even specific meditations that emphasize gratitude as a means to inspire and motivate practitioners. I believe the message is to appreciate what you have now, to enjoy it and let it be a resource for you—all the while knowing that nothing is permanent. In this way, the things that we appreciate will help sustain us through the difficult times.

We can appreciate what we have now and celebrate the good things in our lives. Open your heart to gratitude. Pay attention to the feeling in your being that arises when you feel grateful. You can open to gratitude and tap it in, letting the feeling it awakens in you strengthen and integrate. In this way it will become more accessible to you in daily life.

✳ Tapping In Gratitude

1. Find a quiet place to sit where you won't be disturbed. Take a few moments to quiet your mind and

come to the present moment. Take some deep, relaxing breaths, filling your belly, chest, and throat; hold your breath a moment, then slowly let it out, relaxing with the exhalation. Take another deep breath, and then slowly let it out. When you feel yourself present, reflect on what you feel grateful about in your life. Review your life. You can focus on people you feel grateful for. You can think about things you have that you enjoy. You can think about your health. You might think about capacities you have such as the ability to appreciate beauty, music, or art. You can focus on gratitude for intellectual, creative, or physical abilities.

2. When you find something you feel grateful about, put your attention there. Amplify the sensory information. Really experience the feelings associated with it. If there are memories associated with it, bring them in as well. When you have a feeling of gratitude, even a little bit, begin to tap. Tap 6 to 12 times at first, then stop and see how you feel. If you want to tap longer to continue to strengthen the positive feeling, you can continue. Tap as long as it feels positive. If your mind should drift to other memories, stop tapping, and return to the thing you feel grateful for. Think of something else if you cannot get the feeling back using the image with which you began.

3. Think of something else you feel grateful for. Again, when you have a strong feeling for it, tap 6 to 12 times. Stop and check in to see how it feels. If it continues to be positive, tap until you feel complete.

4. Continue to think of things you appreciate. Each time you find something to be grateful for, focus there, and tap to strengthen it. If you are feeling down, look for even the smallest things— an appreciation of music or a meal you enjoyed recently. Keep going, tapping in gratitude as long as you like. This can take a few minutes or longer.

You might use this practice to begin or end your day, tapping in gratitude as a morning prayer or meditation. You can spend time doing a life review, beginning at birth with a focus on gratitude. Each time you find something to appreciate, tap a few times to strengthen it. I appreciate being born. I appreciate my mother's sacrifice to give birth to me. I appreciate all those who helped in my care as a baby. I appreciate my education, my teachers, having books to read, and so on.

USING GRATITUDE TO RELEASE THE PAST

Ruth was feeling overwhelmed by memories from her traumatic childhood. She was dreaming about the past and experiencing flashbacks and intrusive images. Even though her childhood was fraught with violence, her adult life was not that way at all. Ruth had married a man who loved her, and she had two children she was close to. She had friends and a career she enjoyed. There was nothing in her current life that reflected the traumatic experience of her childhood.

In order to help Ruth focus and connect more deeply with the here and now, I asked her to think about all the things she appreciated in her current life. What are the good things in your life? What are you grateful for? She began to list for me the things she appreciated. I then asked her to take a few moments to close her eyes and go inside, to take some deep, relaxing breaths and slowly let them out. When she indicated to me that she was feeling more present, I asked her to bring to her awareness the things she had mentioned that she appreciated from her current life: her family, friends, job, good health, peace in her life, and so on. "When you feel the feeling of gratitude, begin to tap. Continue tapping as long as it feels good," I told her. She crossed her arms in front of her chest and began to tap on her shoulders using the butterfly hug. As she tapped, I could see her shoulders release and her breathing become deeper and more regular. After tapping for a while, she opened her eyes. She told me that she felt much better. She *did* have a good life now. There were so many things she appreciated. She no longer felt the past activated; the past felt like the past.

Precious Life Meditation

There is a Tibetan Buddhist meditation that is used as an antidote to depression and hopelessness that focuses on appreciating our precious life. I learned this meditation in 1975 at a retreat with Lama Thubten Yeshe and Lama

Thubten Zopa. In this meditation you focus on all of the factors that you have been born with that are rare and precious, such as having a body and mind that is functioning, having enough to eat and drink to sustain you, living in a country where you have many freedoms, and so on. When you look at how so much of the world lives, you can see how privileged we are in the West. I have modified the meditation I was taught to make it applicable to a wider audience and added the tapping to it to help strengthen and integrate the feeling and understanding this meditation elicits in the practitioner.

✳ Tapping In Gratitude for Your Precious Life

1. Begin by finding a quiet place to sit. Bring your attention to your breath. Take some deep, relaxing breaths. Feel yourself present. Spend as much time as you need to bring yourself to the here and now.

2. Bring to mind all the good qualities and advantages of your life, such as the following: You have an intelligent mind, loving heart, and healthy body. You have friends and family you care about. You have the good fortune to live in a country comparatively free of social and political oppression. You have countless opportunities to pursue your creative, intellectual, and social interests. You have the possibility to travel if you want to. Compared to many in the world, you enjoy a good standard of living. You have the freedom to explore spirituality in whatever form you are drawn to.

3. Think of how few people on earth have the freedoms you enjoy. In many parts of the world, people don't have the possibility to travel, study, work, enjoy life, or freely practice their choice of spirituality or religion as you do.

4. As you consider this, realize how rare and precious your life is. Let yourself appreciate the value of this life. As you contemplate your precious life and can *feel* gratitude, begin to tap, right-left, right-left. Tap as long as it continues to feel positive and the good feeling strengthens. When you're done, sit with the feeling of gratitude.

Favorite Things

Remember the song "My Favorite Things" from *The Sound of Music*? The Von Trapp children are frightened during a thunderstorm. In order to help them cope, Maria, their nanny, teaches the children that they can focus on their favorite things to lift their spirits. Later they will sing the song to help them when they are fleeing the Nazis. She begins with describing resources that lift her spirits: "Raindrops on roses and whiskers on kittens." Then she tells us how she uses these resources, and how they help her: "When I'm feeling sad, I simply remember my favorite things, and then I don't feel so bad." As schmaltzy as it is, this technique of focusing the mind on positive, uplifting images can work to change our state of mind.

When we feel low, we can get stuck in memories that are negative and painful. We seem caught in a cycle of thoughts that reinforce our depression, sadness, or feelings of being stuck and ineffective. It can be difficult to break out of this cycle. By focusing on and tapping in our favorite things, we can get out of the negative loop and connect to what is positive and enlivening within us. We have the power to change the channel in our mind if we put attention and effort into it.

Your favorite things might include playing with a litter of puppies or kittens, remembering the joyful expression on your child's face after he or she accomplished something, performing music you love, holding your newborn babies, your wedding day, beach sunrises and sunsets, beautiful gardens, viewing wildlife, recalling special childhood memories, playing a sport you love, time spent with friends and family, savoring a favorite meal, or watching great performances of any kind. There are numerous memories and images that inspire a feeling of joy and lightness of being when I think of them.

✳ Tapping In Favorite Things

1. Spend a few moments thinking of *your* favorite things—places you love, things you love to do, imagery that puts a smile on your face.

2. Enhance your senses. What are you seeing? What are you hearing? What sensations do you notice? What

are you smelling? Are you tasting anything? Notice how you feel when you think of one of your favorite things. What does your body feel like? Pay attention.

3. When the image is strong and you have fully positive feelings, begin to tap. Tap 6 to 12 times, and see how you feel. If the positive feeling is getting stronger, or if you are having more happy memories with positive, uplifting imagery, you can tap longer.

4. Now bring up another favorite thing. When you feel it strongly, tap it as well. Continue to think of favorite things and tap them in until you feel complete and have noticed a change in your state of mind to one that is lighter, more optimistic.

5. When you are feeling down or depressed, imagine your favorite things, and tap them in. Notice how you feel. Continue to think of favorite things and tap as long as it remains positive to do so.

Developing a List of Your Favorite Things

• Make a list of your favorite things. Write them down. Notice how you feel when you make the list. Savor the good feelings. Tap to increase and strengthen the feelings.

- Draw pictures of your favorite things. After you have drawn the pictures, take in the feeling of being uplifted. Tap to strengthen and integrate the feelings.

- Find photographs, images from magazines, or postcards of your favorite things. Make a collage of these images that you can look at when you wish to be uplifted.

USING FAVORITE THINGS DURING A DIFFICULT TIME

Peter was struggling with depression. He was embroiled in a bitter divorce and custody battle that was wearing him down. He had a hard time getting out of bed in the morning and felt like he was dragging throughout the day. It was difficult for him to find pleasure in his life.

During a therapy session we explored things that he loved to do, things that lifted his spirit. Peter's creative outlet was playing the saxophone. He loved to play improvisational jazz. I asked him to remember a time when he was immersed in his music, a time when he felt creative. He quickly came up with a time when he was playing with a group of friends. They fell into a groove together, and hours passed without anyone noticing. As he remembered this experience, evoking his sense memories, he tapped on his knees to strengthen and integrate the experience. He tapped for several minutes, a smile forming on his face.

After this, I asked him for something else he loved to do. He told me he enjoyed cooking and entertaining friends. I asked him to recall a time when he made a meal and felt happy. He brought to mind a time when he made a feast for a friend's birthday. A group of friends gathered at his home to enjoy the meal. As he recalled this time, he resumed tapping on his knees. Tapping caused him to associate with other times he had enjoyed cooking. At the end of the session he felt uplifted and renewed.

Experiences of Awe and Wonder

Advaita Vedanta master Jean Klein advised his students to pay attention to moments of awe. He said that these moments provide us with glimpses of the absolute, our everabiding presence. These can include the births of children, experiences in nature, or even hearing a special piece of music. These experiences are reminders of something that is much larger than us. Recalling these experiences and adding tapping to strengthen and integrate them can help us reconnect with that vaster understanding and help us view our troubles within a broader perspective.

I have had many experiences that evoked wonder, especially in nature. One of the most powerful happened a few years ago on a trip with my family to the south rim of the Grand Canyon. The first day we drove to the different vista points and gazed out at the great expanse of colored rock. I was deeply impressed by the immensity of the canyon, which was beyond my mind's capacity to grasp. Jean Klein used to tell us to let our energy bodies expand to fill the space in front of us and then see how it acted on us. Following his advice, I imagined my energy filling the canyon. How open and exhilarated I felt! But what happened the next day had an even greater impact on me.

The following morning we returned to the canyon, but were disappointed to find it completely obscured by clouds. It was as if the canyon in all its grandeur had magically vanished. My husband and I followed the short trail to the rim and peered out into a sea of whiteness. Then, slowly, delicately, like rising smoke, the clouds began to part. As the wispy veils lifted, the canyon was revealed to us in its magnificence, an expanse so vast we were awestruck. Then, just as suddenly as it had appeared, it vanished, covered again by the flowing sea of whiteness. Then, stillness. With this glimpse of the infinite, our minds stopped, and we dropped into the timeless. We stood transfixed in silence for several minutes, resonating with the sacred moment.

I had another experience of awe during the time I was writing this book. My husband and I were on the upper deck of our Mexican casa on the Morua Estero near the Sea of Cortez, gazing out at the brilliant star-filled sky, when a meteor flashed a brilliant arc across the sky, trailing a tail of white light behind it. It was low in the sky and seemed to linger in its descent before it vanished into emptiness. My husband and I both saw it, and in that moment, time stood still. We were again struck silent in astonishment and awe. It was an experience that took us out of our minds, gifted us with something much greater than we are.

We can recall and tap experiences such as these. They can be recalled to inspire us and provide a broader context. What are some experiences you have had that inspired awe, wonder, and astonishment? Take some time to review those times in your life. As you do so, notice how you feel. How do these memories act on your whole system?

✳ Tapping In Experiences of Awe and Wonder

1. Sit quietly, close your eyes, and go inside. Bring yourself to the present moment. Take some deep breaths and slowly release them. Relax and release with each exhalation. If you like, you can imagine that you are in your safe/peaceful place. Take as long as you like to relax and feel at ease.

2. Bring to mind a time when you felt an experience of awe or astonishment, a time when you were struck by something beautiful or amazing, an experience that took you out of your ordinary way of perceiving things.

3. When the memory comes to you, spend some time enhancing your senses. What are you seeing? Look around you. What sounds do you hear? What do you smell? What sensations do you feel on your skin?

4. When you have evoked a strong sense of the memory, begin to tap. Tap 6 to 12 times. If the feeling is continuing to strengthen, you can tap longer. Tap until it feels complete.

5. Now sit a while longer with the feeling of the experience. Savor it. Allow it to give you its gift.

6. If you like, you can tap in a cue word with the image. Find a word associated with the experience. Tap as you imagine the scene, and repeat the word to yourself.

7. You can recall the image with the cue word and tap whenever you want to elicit a sense of the experience.

Beauty

Jean Klein would also advise his students to "live in beauty," and then see how it "acted" on us. Our environment affects us without our being aware of it. For many of us, traffic, honking cars, loud voices, grey grimy buildings, and streets littered with trash are jarring to our nervous systems. In defense, we pull our energy inside, contract and harden ourselves. In contrast, beauty inspires us, lifts us up, and opens us. Beauty resonates with our deepest nature, our highest self. Beauty recognizes itself. Our whole being resonates with beauty. We naturally expand when we are touched by beauty. Beauty can be found in many places, including nature, art, architecture, and music. You may even experience beauty in a large city.

Try this experiment with yourself. Bring up an image or memory of being in an unattractive environment, such as an industrial urban area where there is a lot of pollution, noise, and traffic. Notice how you feel when you evoke this memory. How does your body react? What do you feel in your heart center? Now think of something you find to be beautiful. It can be a place in nature, a work of art, or a piece of music. Pay attention to how you feel. What do you notice in your body? How does your heart feel? Are you expanded or contracted?

It is important to bring beauty into one's life. Even a few flowers in a drab room can be uplifting. What do you find that is beautiful? What inspires you?

✳ Tapping In Beauty

1. Find a quiet place to sit. Bring yourself to the present moment. Feel yourself sitting. Take some deep, relaxing breaths.

2. When you are relaxed, bring to mind something beautiful. It can be a work of art, music, a scene from nature, or anything that inspires you.

3. When you have found it, open your senses. What are you seeing, hearing, smelling, tasting, sensing?

4. How does your body feel when you think of this beautiful thing?

5. When you are experiencing good feelings, begin to tap. Tap 6 to 12 times, right-left, right-left. If the feeling is getting stronger you can continue. Stop when it feels complete.

6. If you like, you can bring up something else that is beautiful and tap it in as well.

Joy

What brings you joy? When have you felt joy in your life? Joy bubbles up from our inner wellspring and bursts forth like a fountain evoking tears and laughter. Joy opens our hearts. Memories of joy can help inspire and uplift us during times when we are feeling down.

If you have difficulty thinking of a time when you felt joy, you can think of someone you know who is joyful. When my sister thinks about her exuberant two-year-old grandson, she beams, her mood immediately lightening. You can think of a person you know or even a character from a movie, book, or TV show. When I think of Charlie Chaplin, Robin Williams, or Gene Kelly in *Singin' in the Rain*, I feel joy. You can even bring to mind animals that evoke the feeling, such as frolicking otters or soaring eagles.

✳ Tapping In Joy

1. Find a place to sit quietly. Bring your awareness to the present moment. Feel yourself sitting. When you are in the here and now, bring up a memory of when you felt joy. It can be a time from your adulthood or from childhood. You can also think of someone you know, a character from a movie or book, or even an animal that makes you feel happy.

2. When you have the image, open your senses. What are you seeing? What do you hear? What do you smell? What sensations do you feel on your skin? What do you feel in your body?

3. When you can feel joy, even just a little, begin to tap. Tap right-left, right-left, 6 to 12 times. Tap longer if it feels good and the resource continues to strengthen.

4. Savor the feeling of joy. Let it permeate your body. Allow your heart to open and receive it.

5. If you want to continue, think of something else that evokes joy, and tap it in. Continue bringing up joyful images or memories and tapping as long as they are positive and feel good to you.

Humor and Laughter

Laughter can lift our spirits, creating a sense of well-being, and even can help to heal us physically. The writer Norman Cousins cured himself of a rare form of degenerative arthritis by learning how to laugh. He read funny books, watched comedies on TV, and spent time laughing each day. He wrote about his experience in his book *Anatomy of an Illness.* We don't have to have a rare disease to spend time watching movies and TV shows that make us laugh, to read funny books, and to recall times that made us laugh. When we laugh, our whole system opens up, and we feel a release. Laughter is a good antidote to depression and to feeling stuck in our lives.

✳ Tapping In Humorous Times

1. Think of a time when you laughed hard, a time when you were struck by something really funny. It can be something funny that happened to you or someone you know, something funny you read, a joke, a movie, or a TV show.

2. Now immerse yourself in the memory. What was happening? Who were you with? Bring it back as strongly as you can.

3. When you feel lighter, begin to tap. Tap right-left, right-left, 6 to 12 times. Tap longer if it continues to feel good, and stop if for any reason it doesn't .

4. If other funny memories come up, you can tap as you recall them, too. Continue to tap as long as you feel good.

If you are watching a funny movie or something humorous on TV, you can tap during the funny parts to take in the benefits of the experience more fully. You might even prescribe yourself funny movies as a way to lift your spirits. What are your favorites? Tap and laugh as you watch. If you are embarrassed about looking weird, you can subtly tap your toes.

The following is a funny story from my childhood that I think about when I want to lift my spirits. Perhaps it can inspire you to think of humorous stories from your life that you can use as resources to tap in.

One evening when I was about ten, my parents went out and left my sister, brother, and me with a new babysitter, a proper woman in her middle years my mother had found through an agency. Before leaving, my mother gave her instructions about what to feed us for dinner. She told her that there was hamburger meat in the freezer that should be defrosted and prepared.

That evening, my sister, brother, and I sat down to eat our dinner prepared by the babysitter. I poured ketchup on my plate and dipped a piece of meat patty into it. I took a bite of the meat, chewed for a moment, then quickly spit it out. It tasted terrible. I was happy to be sent to my room rather than eat it. But my sister and brother remained at the table, their plates of food in front of them. Because my sister did not want to be in trouble, she obediently choked down the food, swigging lots of milk to help it go down. But my little brother actually liked it. He cleaned his plate without complaint and even asked for seconds.

When my parents returned that evening the babysitter told on me. That's when my mother remembered the year-old package of dog food neatly wrapped in butcher paper in the back of the freezer. My sister may not think this is a funny story, but when I remember our kid brother asking for a second helping of dog food, I never fail to giggle.

Inspiration

We can tap in inspiration as a resource to lift our spirits. We can bring to mind times in our lives when we were inspired or think of others we find inspiring. What inspires you? Who has inspired you? Have you read or heard any stories that have inspired you? Whom do you admire—Gandhi, Martin Luther King Jr., Nelson Mandela, Helen Keller, Jane Goodall, Albert Schweitzer, Maya Angelou, Abraham Lincoln, Warren Buffet, Bill Gates, Franklin Delano Roosevelt, Eleanor Roosevelt, Mother Teresa, John Muir? You can be inspired by people you know personally or those you have heard about. They can be historical, political, spiritual, business, or sports figures, or they can be characters from books or movies. They can even be ordinary people you know or have read about who have inspired you.

✳ Tapping In Inspiration

1. Find a place to sit quietly. Close your eyes and go inside. Bring yourself to the present moment.

2. Now think of a time when you felt inspired. Alternatively, you can bring to mind someone who inspires you. It can be someone you know or someone you have heard or read about.

3. When you think about inspiration, what image comes to mind? Notice what you see. If it is a memory of being inspired, bring back the sensory details of the experience as much as you can. If you are thinking of a person who inspires you, bring that person to mind as strongly as you can. Represent him or her in a way that evokes the feeling of inspiration.

4. Once you have the image and can feel the feelings associated with inspiration, begin to tap. Tap 6 to 12 times, right-left, right-left. Stop for a moment and check in to see how you are feeling. If you feel good, continue to tap. Keep tapping as long as it feels positive and the feeling of inspiration continues to strengthen.

5. You can bring up another resource that inspires you if you wish, and tap that in as well.

6. Imagine taking these inspiring resources with you into a future situation. If you are facing an obstacle, tap in your resources to give yourself needed strength.

Suggestions for Developing Inspirational Resources

• Draw your experiences of being inspired, or draw your inspirational figures. Add in whatever visual details will enhance your experience. After you have drawn them, feel the feelings of inspiration that are evoked, and then tap to strengthen and integrate them.

- Find photographs or pictures from magazines of your inspirational resources. Tap in the feelings or experiences they evoke in you, and then place them where you can see them to continue to inspire you.

- Make a collage of your inspirational resources. Tap it in, and keep it in a place where you will see it.

Freedom and Expansion

When you are feeling stuck, stagnant, or without per-spective in your life, you can tap in the feeling of freedom to help open your mind and make room for new possibilities. You can use a memory of having felt open and free, or think of someone who demonstrates this quality. You can also bring to mind an animal or another image from nature that speaks of freedom to you.

What evokes the feeling of freedom for you? What do you think of when you imagine expansion, liberation? Is there a place you've been that has a vast vista? Have you flown an airplane and felt free? Is there a sporting activ-ity that evokes this feeling? Have you had a dream that inspires a feeling of freedom? There are many images I can bring to mind that evoke the feeling of freedom for me. When I imagine watching the vultures soar above the hills near my home in California, gracefully riding the currents of air, implicitly trusting that their wings will support them, I feel like I am flying with them. I feel light, happy, a little giddy. Imagining their wings spread wide, I feel my heart open, too. I often dream about flying; it's my favorite dream. Unencumbered by the weight of my body, I am free to go where I please. These dreams are exhilarating. I can also remember hiking high into the mountains to viewpoints from which I could see vast distances, and driving on the highway through the desert where the sky is wide open and the landscape uncluttered.

✳ Tapping In Freedom and Expansion

1. Close your eyes and go inside. Bring your awareness to your breath. Take some deep breaths in, and then slowly let them out. Relax and let go of all tension with each exhalation. When you feel yourself present, think of a time when you felt free and open, a time when your body felt expanded, unfettered. It can even include a dream you have had that evoked the feeling of freedom. You can also think of someone you know who has this quality or of an animal, an image, or an experience from nature.

2. When the image comes to you, open your senses. What are you seeing? Notice any visual details that help bring the experience more fully awake for you. What are you hearing? Smelling? Tasting? What do you feel on your skin? As you evoke this image, how does your body feel?

3. When you feel open, free, and expanded, begin to tap. Tap 6 to 12 times, right-left, right-left. Stop and

check in with how you are feeling. If it feels good, and you want to tap some more, you can continue. Tap as long as it feels good to you. Stop when it feels complete.

4. You may also tap in a cue word with the image. As you see the image and feel the experience of freedom, say to yourself a cue word that goes with the image (for example, "flying") and tap for a short time.

5. When you are finished, sit for a few moments savoring the feeling of freedom and expansion you have evoked. Remember that you can elicit this feeling with the image and cue word whenever you like.

CHAPTER 17

Spiritual and Wisdom Resources

We are the mirror as well as the face in it.

—RUMI

SPIRITUAL AND WISDOM resources can be evoked and tapped in to help support us in a variety of ways. These resources provide a larger context within which we can view our lives and our problems. They can help us feel more connected to our spirituality and deepen our spiritual practice. They can sustain, empower, and inspire us. Evoking spiritual resources can remind us of our true nature, our ground of being. In this chapter you will find a large selection of spiritual and wisdom resources to choose from.

Sacred Place

A variant on the safe/peaceful place resource is the sacred place. Instead of focusing on the sense of safety, the emphasis is on the feeling of sacredness in the space, a place where you have a feeling of spirituality. The sacred place can be a place you have been to or a place you can imagine. In this place you feel peaceful, but you also feel a sense of something larger than yourself. Here you can imagine meeting a wise figure who can give you advice. This special place can be contacted when you desire to open to your creativity or wisdom. Examples of sacred places might include Chartre Cathedral in France, the Hopi mesas, a Pueblo kiva, a meditation cave in the Himalayas, a meditation hall with a spiritual teacher, or a sacred landscape, such as the Grand Canyon.

 ## Tapping In Your Sacred Place

1. Close your eyes and go inside. Spend a few moments bringing yourself to the present. Feel yourself sitting. Now take some deep, full breaths. Allow yourself to relax and let go as you slowly exhale.

2. When you feel relaxed, imagine yourself in a sacred place. It can be a place you have been before, a place you have read about, or a place you create in your imagination. It can be a physical structure or a place in nature. Maybe you have visited this place in a dream. In this place you feel peaceful and sense a beautiful

spiritual vibration. It is your sanctuary. You can invite spiritual figures to be there with you, or you can be there by yourself. You can create the space however you like. Feel the sense of profound peace in this special place. In this place you can contact your higher wisdom and your source of creativity. Your sanctuary can open you to a broader perspective on your life.

3. When you have found your sacred place, notice what you see there. Look around. What do you hear? What do you smell? What does your body feel?

4. When you have a strong feeling of your sacred place, begin to tap. Tap right-left, right-left, 6 to 12 times. If the feeling gets stronger, tap longer.

5. Spend as much time as you would like in your sanctuary. Remember, this special place is always here for you when you need it.

Spiritual Figures

Have you had a special connection with a spiritual figure through a religious/spiritual experience or a dream? Is there someone or something you associate with spiritual energy or your own spirituality? These figures can be called upon during times of fear or anxiety to provide comfort and support. When we are feeling alone and are having difficulty coping, we can evoke and tap in these figures to help us. We can tap them in any time we want to feel more connected to our spirituality. I know people who have tapped in Jesus, Mary, Kwan Yin, the Buddha, Tara, the Goddess, Native American wise men and women, power animals, angelic beings, spirit guides, and spiritual teachers. It helps to remember that our spiritual figures are always close at hand; we need only focus inward, recall them, and tap to increase our felt connection with them. I have received teachings and initiations from several awakened masters, including Lama Thubten Yeshe, His Holiness the Dalai Lama, and Jean Klein. I have also received transmission and initiation into the Tibetan deities Tara, Chenrezig, Vajrapani, and Vajrasattva. I can tap in each of them to serve as spiritual resource figures.

In Tibetan Buddhist practices, deities are visualized and their attributes focused on in order to cultivate those qualities in the practitioner. The attributes of the different deities are understood to represent essential qualities that reside within each human being. The practices involve identifying oneself completely—body, mind, and spirit—with an enlightened being. Each deity is a manifestation of a specific quality, such as compassion, wisdom, or power, but each also represents the total experience of enlightenment.

Before deity practice begins in Tibetan Buddhism, practitioners receive an initiation and empowerment from a teacher who provides them with a direct experience of the essential qualities of the deity. In this way the meditator has a spiritual familiarity with the deity that is felt in the body. It is also crucial to this work that we have a body-based feeling of the resource before we tap it in. An idea or image won't integrate into our systems; we must feel the resource physically. The feeling of the resource can come in many ways—from a spiritual experience, dream, vision, visitation of some kind, or simply a felt connection with the figure. For example, Tibetan Buddhist practitioners may imagine the deity Tara, the female expression of compassion, with visual and sensory detail, and generate in themselves the feeling she evokes. They train their minds to cultivate different essential qualities through their practice, after which they utilize these qualities in daily life. In such a way we can take some of the ideas from Tibetan Buddhism and utilize them in our resource tapping.

I met Lama Yeshe, my spiritual teacher, when I was twenty years old. Over a period of nine years I had the opportunity to receive teachings and initiations, and attend several retreats with him. Lama Yeshe was an extraordinary human being. Small in stature, head shaved, he wore the orange robes of a Tibetan monk. He had an enormous smile that displayed slightly crooked front teeth and a laugh so exuberant that it would fill a lecture hall with joy and hilarity. When I met with him privately, he would take my hands in his and always ask about my family. I have never felt more loved by anyone in my life.

To use Lama Yeshe as a spiritual resource, I imagine him in front of me, sitting cross-legged in his orange robes. He gazes at me with a loving expression, his palms together in a prayer mudra. As I see him, I feel the love from him emanating toward me. As I take in the love, I feel my heart expand. I receive the essential qualities of wisdom and compassion from Lama Yeshe—qualities that are no different from my own, which are only less awakened than his. I can even imagine these qualities or energies radiating out from Lama Yeshe's form and entering me through my head, heart, and solar plexus. As these qualities enter me, and I can feel them, I begin to tap. I tap on my knees, right-left, right-left. I continue to tap as long as the feeling of wisdom and compassion grows and is completely positive. When this is complete, I spend a few moments sitting, allowing myself to savor the feeling. I remind myself that I can contact the Lama Yeshe within myself whenever I need to.

 ## Tapping In Spiritual Figures

1. Close your eyes and go inside. Take some deep, relaxing breaths. Let go and release with each exhalation. When you feel more present and relaxed, imagine going to your sacred place or sanctuary. Tap as you feel yourself in your sacred place.

2. Bring to mind someone or something you associate with spirituality. It can be someone you have met, someone you have read about, someone or something from a dream, or a figure such as Jesus or Kwan Yin. If you had

a spiritual experience that involved the spiritual figure, recall the experience as completely as you can.

3. After bringing the figure to mind, focus on visual details. What does your spiritual figure look like? What is he or she wearing? What expression is on your spiritual figure's face?

4. If it helps you to feel the spirituality of the figure in your body, fill in more sensory detail. Notice any sounds, smells, or bodily sensations. Feel the spiritual vibration of the figure. Sense his or her qualities.

5. As you imagine the figure and feel the spiritual qualities, begin to tap. Tap right-left, right-left, 6 to 12 times. Tap longer if the resource strengthens and remains positive.

6. If you would like, you can imagine light or energy of the color you associate with the spiritual qualities of your figure radiating out from his or her forehead, throat, and heart centers and entering your forehead, throat, and heart centers. When you can see and feel this, tap. Tap as long as it continues to feel positive. You are taking in the positive qualities of your spiritual resource.

7. Imagine your being filling with these qualities. Remember that these are your own inherent qualities. They have always resided within you.

8. Whenever you want to connect to the spiritual resource that is associated with this spiritual figure, you can imagine the figure, feel the associated feelings, and tap.

USING A SPIRITUAL FIGURE TO HELP
RECONNECT TO SPIRITUALITY

Pamela was struggling with a feeling of disconnection from her spirituality. She felt there was something wrong, that she was missing something important. She'd had many meaningful spiritual experiences as a child that, while very significant to her at the time, now felt distant. The most profound experience occurred during a time of trouble in her family. Her alcoholic father was raging, scaring her to death. She walked into the living room and suddenly had a vision of the Virgin Mary emanating golden light and love. This vision had deeply moved and comforted her. We decided to tap in this childhood spiritual experience to help her.

I asked her to close her eyes and go inside, to spend a few moments relaxing, coming to the present moment. I then invited her to remember the time when she was a little girl and Mary had appeared to her. "Remember how you felt when that happened. Can you feel it? Do you have a sense of the experience?" When she nodded her head, I instructed her to either tap on her knees or to cross her arms across her chest and tap on her shoulders. "Tap to strengthen the feeling. Tap as long as it feels good." Pamela was silent for several minutes, tapping on her shoulders. As she tapped I could see her body relax, the tension on her face release, and a soft smile appear on her lips.

When she opened her eyes, she exclaimed, "I could feel it! She was profoundly compassionate. The vision was so strong. I can feel it in here." She pointed to her heart. As a result of tapping in this experience, Pamela had a stronger connection to an important spiritual resource and was able to use tapping to reconnect to it when she felt the need.

Higher Power

Many people relate to the concept of a higher power. A higher power provides wisdom, guidance, and a broader perspective. You may have had an experience of a higher power. It may have come while in nature, during meditation or prayer, or during a time of great duress. Contact with a higher power provides comfort and a sense that there is something much greater than oneself directing the unfolding of one's life. Learning to listen and attune to the wisdom expressed through the higher power provides a foundation for healing work. All the twelve-step programs draw from this understanding.

We can contact a sense of our higher power, and tap it in to strengthen the feeling and make it more accessible to us. In so doing we can call on it to provide wisdom and direction to our lives.

✳ Tapping In Your Higher Power

1. Close your eyes and go inside. Take a few moments to find that quiet place inside yourself. You might take

some long, deep breaths to calm your mind. When you are quiet inside, imagine going to your safe/peaceful place. This is your special place where you are at ease and can be fully who you are. Spend as much time as you need in your peaceful sanctuary.

2. Now open yourself to experiencing your higher power. You may have a direct experience of it in the moment, or you may recall a time when you had a strong feeling of it. Allow yourself to experience it in whatever form it takes.

3. When you have a sense or feeling of your higher power, begin to tap. Tap 6 to 12 times. If you would like to tap longer, you may continue as long as it feels positive, and the contact with your higher power strengthens.

4. If you have a problem for which you need guidance, a request, or a question, you can speak to your higher power.

5. Now listen for the response. Be open to receiving it in the way in which it comes. You may receive it in words, pictures, or feelings.

6. When you receive the message, begin to tap. Tap as long as it feels positive.

7. Imagine what your life would be like if you followed the guidance of your higher power. Tap as you imagine it.

8. Remember that you can contact your higher power at any time. It is always with you. You are never separate from it.

The Essential Spiritual Self

The essential spiritual self is the essence of who you are, a core of goodness that has been there all your life. This is the part of you that has never been touched by any of the bad things that might have happened to you. It has always remained with you in the background. You can contact it, tap it in, and use it as a resource for wisdom and support when you need it.

✳ Tapping In the Essential Spiritual Self

1. Find a quiet place to sit where you won't be disturbed for a while. Close your eyes and go inside. Feel yourself sitting. Take some deep breaths in and slowly let them out. Relax and let go with each exhalation. As you take another deep breath, imagine breathing up from the center of the earth, and then release your breath back down into the earth. Let go of all the tension in your body and mind as you exhale. Take some more deep breaths, relaxing with the exhalation.

2. When you feel relaxed, imagine going to your safe/peaceful place. Take as much time as you need to go there. Look around—what you see? What do you hear? What bodily sensations are you aware of? How do you feel in your special place? When you feel good and relaxed, tap a few times to increase the feeling.

3. Now, in your special place, allow yourself to connect to your essential spiritual self. This essential part of yourself was there before you were born and has been

there all your life. This is the part of you that has been with you through all you have experienced in your life, yet has not been touched by any of it. This part of you is pure, good, innocent, wise, and resilient. This is the core of your being.

4. When you have a sense of your essential spiritual self, begin to tap. Tap 6 to 12 times, and then stop to check in with yourself. If the connection and feeling is strengthening, tap some more. Tap as long as it feels positive.

5. If a name for your essential spiritual self comes up, take note of it and tap it in.

6. If it seems right, allow an image to arise of your essential spiritual self. If no image comes up, that is fine. If you have an image and would like to strengthen your connection to it, tap 6 to 12 times.

7. Remember that your essential spiritual self is always with you. You can contact it whenever you need to. All you have to do is imagine it, say its name, and tap.

Wise Beings

The image of a man or woman of wisdom can be used as a resource to inspire, support, and help connect you to your own source of wisdom. Wisdom is an innate quality that resides within each of us. But like the sun covered by clouds, our wisdom is often obscured by our conditioning. The wise being resource represents a being that is integrated and whole, wise and compassionate. When you think of a wise being, what comes up for you? These images can include people you know or have heard or read about or figures from dreams, your imagination, or guided imagery. They can include religious or spiritual figures, mythological beings, animals, or images from movies or books. When I think of wise beings, Lama Yeshe, Jean Klein, His Holiness the Dalai Lama, and Ramana Maharshi come up for me. These are all sages whose teaching has inspired me in my life. Some people have used Aslan, the wise, majestic lion from the *Chronicles of Narnia*; Gandalf the wizard from *Lord of the Rings*; and even Walter Cronkite! I have had several clients reveal to me that as children, compassionate, wise "beings of light" would visit them. Sometimes these beings would teach them things, and other times they simply conveyed a sense of peace through their presence. With my guidance these clients were able to tap in these beings as resources. Have you experienced a wise being? Do you know someone who is wise? It is essential that when you think of the being, you have a felt sense of his or her quality of wisdom.

✳ Tapping In a Wise Being

1. Close your eyes and go inside. Take some time to relax your mind, and bring yourself to the present moment.

2. When you feel yourself present, bring to mind a wise being. It can be someone you know, have met, in

person or in the media. It can be someone from history, someone you have read about, or someone from a movie or book. It can be a person, an animal, or a mythological being. It can also be a spiritual being.

3. When you have an image of the wise being, notice what he or she looks like. What expression is on his or her face? Can you feel this person is wise and compassionate?

4. When you have a strong feeling for this being, begin to tap. Tap 6 to 12 times, then stop. Check in to see how you are feeling. If it feels positive, tap some more. Tap as long as it feels good.

5. If you would like, bring to mind another wise being.

6. What does this being look like? What expression does he or she have?

7. When you feel this being's wisdom and compassion, begin to tap. Tap 6 to 12 times, or longer if it continues to feel positive.

8. Repeat this process for as many wise figures as you would like.

Spiritual Experiences

Many of us have had spiritual experiences that have had an impact on our lives. These experiences inspire awe and a sense of something much larger than ourselves. Though at the time we are profoundly moved by these experiences, after a while the effect they have on on our lives diminishes, we lose our connection to them, and our memory fades. Many people have spiritual experiences when they are children. Sometimes these experiences are very confusing because the child has no context for understanding what has happened. Sometimes it is the parents who lack the context for the child's experiences and are frightened by what their children tell them. I have heard many stories of parents admonishing their children to never speak of these experiences again.

Spiritual experiences inspire awe, openness, and stillness. Often there is an opening of the heart. Jean Klein used to tell his students to wear these experiences around our necks like an amulet. By staying close to our hearts, they would remain accessible, serving to inspire and guide us. You can strengthen and integrate spiritual experiences by recalling them and tapping. These can include experiences you had during meditation or prayer, in a dream, in nature, or a peak experience during an athletic feat.

Recalling and tapping in a spiritual experience may help you more fully integrate the experience into your life. How did it affect you? What did you learn from it? How would you like to take the essence of the experience into your life now? Remembering your deepest experiences can help you to feel that your life is spiritually oriented, that there is a larger context and meaning. These resources can also be tapped in when we wish to get in touch with a broader perspective in our life. You may not reexperience a spiritual opening, but evoking the memory and tapping may awaken its feeling or flavor so that it is more available to you. These experiences can later be recalled to bring a sense of something larger than yourself and to provide inspiration and support.

✳ Tapping In Spiritual Experiences

1. Close your eyes and go inside. Bring yourself to the present moment. Feel yourself sitting, make contact with the seat. Take some deep breaths, and exhale slowly, letting go and releasing with your breath. Take the time you need to let go and come into the now. You might even tap for a few minutes, right-left, right-left, to calm your mind. If it helps, you can imagine going to your sacred place first.

2. Think of a time when you had a spiritual experience, an experience of something larger than yourself that inspired awe. This can be an experience of opening to a higher consciousness, a spiritual insight, an experience of God or a higher power, or anything you *feel* was spiritual. It can include a vision or dream or an experience in nature. You may have experienced it in your adulthood or even in childhood. Invite in whatever comes to you.

3. Now see if you can recall the experience as much as you can. Where are you? What are you doing? If it applies to this experience, bring in sensory information. What are you seeing, hearing, smelling, feeling in your body? Notice how you feel inside.

4. Now open to the experience. Allow it to unfold in you. Take in the information it offers you. Let it fill you with its flavor, the essence of its message.

5. When you have a feeling for the experience, begin to tap. Tap right-left, right-left, 6 to 12 times. If the feeling continues to strengthen and integrate, continue tapping until the experience feels complete to you.

6. Sit for some moments with the feeling. Remember that you can recall this experience and tap to contact and strengthen it whenever you feel the need.

USING A SPIRITUAL EXPERIENCE TO HELP RECONNECT TO SPIRITUALITY

Eva felt disconnected from her spirituality. She told me that she'd had a spiritual connection with God in the past, but could no longer feel it in the same way. She felt stuck in her life and yearned for a sense of being connected to something greater than herself. I thought that we might be able to access a memory of her experience, even just a taste of it, and then strengthen and integrate it by using tapping.

I asked her to close her eyes and go inside, to take a few moments to relax her mind and bring herself to the present. When she felt relaxed, I asked her to bring up the memory of a time when she felt connected to

God. I asked her where she was at the time, what was happening. I asked her to open her senses and to bring back how she had felt. I wanted her to evoke the *feeling* of the experience. She was silent for a few moments, then told me that she was able to recall some of the feeling of a connection to God. I then asked her to tap on her knees, right-left, right-left, and to tap as long as it felt good and the spiritual connection continued to grow.

She tapped for several minutes, and her face had a peaceful expression. Finally she opened her eyes. She told me that her connection to God came back very strongly, almost as strongly as when she'd first experienced it. She recognized that God was always with her and that she could contact this feeling by silently going inside, recalling the memory, and then tapping. As a result of tapping in this spiritual experience, she was able to feel connected to God in a way she hadn't felt in a very long time.

USING A SPIRITUAL EXPERIENCE FROM NATURE TO GAIN PERSPECTIVE AND INSPIRATION

Many years ago, while backpacking high in the Sierra Nevada, Michael had a spiritual experience. The combination of the immense vistas and solid endurance of the mountains struck him like a lightening bolt. In that instant, he dropped into the timeless. Tears streamed down his face. He felt bathed in beauty, his whole system vibrating. The feeling of openness and elation lasted for several days.

At the time I saw him, Michael was struggling in an unhappy relationship and felt dissatisfied in his work. He felt stuck in his life, disconnected from his spiritual perspective.

As a means to inspire him and provide a broader perspective, we decided to tap in the memory of the opening experience he had had in the mountains. I asked him to close his eyes and go inside, to come to the present moment. Then I invited him to bring up the spiritual experience in the mountains.

"Remember what it looked like there. What did you hear? What did you smell? Open your senses as much as possible. What did you feel? When you have a sense of the spiritual experience, let me know."

When he indicated that he had a sense of the experience, I instructed him to tap on his knees for as long as it strengthened, but to stop if it no longer felt good.

Michael was silent for several minutes, tapping on his knees. When he stopped tapping and opened his eyes he told me that he felt wonderful! He felt an expansion in his whole body. He recognized that this feeling was always close at hand. His problems were small compared to the immensity of this experience. I told him that he could recall this experience and others he'd had and tap to contact and strengthen them in the future.

Insights and Life Lessons

We all have untapped wisdom within us. We have learned valuable lessons from our life experiences, but often we don't live our lives from the lessons learned. For some reason the lessons remain unintegrated, stored in compartments in our minds. We do not draw from the information they hold. The good news is that it's possible to better integrate these lessons and to access our wisdom more readily. We need only focus on the insights and wisdom we've gleaned from our lives, and then tap to strengthen and integrate it.

 ## Tapping In Insights and Life Lessons

1. Spend a few moments reflecting on your life. What are the most important insights and lessons you have learned? Have you had experiences of spiritual insight or understanding? Maybe you recall something your father or mother told you as a child that is important to you. If you were going to write down for your children what significant insights and understandings you've had in your life, what would you write? What would you want them to know about? If you have no children, write the list for your loved ones. Take some time to think about and compile this list.

2. Now review what you have written. Take it in. As you take in your own understanding, your own insights about life, tap. Continue to tap as long as it feels positive.

3. Think of a situation in your current life where you might be able to apply some of your wisdom.

4. Imagine bringing your wisdom and understanding to the current problem.

5. If you have a good feeling, and you can feel how your wisdom might help you here, tap. Tap as long as it feels positive.

6. Imagine using your wisdom and understanding in your life. What would your life be like if you lived more from this wisdom? Tap as you imagine it.

7. Remember that these insights are yours. Hold them close at hand. Live by them. Let them guide you.

Spiritual Teachings

Have you been touched by spiritual teaching but have had a hard time living what you have learned? You may have been moved by something you read in a spiritual book. A poem may have struck a chord of understanding, resonating with your deepest self. What are the most important spiritual teachings you have read or received? Jean Klein used to tell his students to "live with the sayings of the guru." In this way the sayings would become our own and orient us in our lives. If we spend some time in contemplation of the spiritual teachings or sayings and then tap them in, we can more fully integrate them into our lives.

* Tapping In Spiritual Teachings

1. Find a quiet place to sit. Close your eyes and go inside yourself. Spend a few moments calming your mind.

2. Review in your mind the most important teachings you have read or received. You might want to focus on just one teaching or saying for the day. What specific teaching would you like to focus on?

3. As you contemplate the teaching and can feel the wisdom in it, tap. Tap as long as it feels positive.

4. Now bring up the next teaching. Tap it in as well.

5. Tap in each of the teachings or sayings you wish to for the day.

6. Imagine taking the teaching into your life. What would your life look like if you lived with this teaching? When you have a strong sense of how your life would be different, tap it in. Tap as long as it feels positive.

Closing Thoughts

The Guest is inside you, and also inside me;
you know the sprout is hidden inside the seed.

—KABIR

IN THIS BOOK, I have introduced you to many resources and ways you can put these resources to work to help you. You have the tools you need, for they are within you. Now it is up to you to use them. Experiment, play with these resources, and discover what works for you. Remember that the main idea with resource tapping is that we are activating positive memory networks as well as our imagination and then integrating them into our whole body-mind system.

The more you use your resources, the more available they will be to you. If you remember and tap in your basic resources, they will be there when you need them. In this way resource tapping becomes a quick and easy method for gaining control over your distress. Over time you will develop confidence in the tools you've tapped in, and they can help you get through many difficulties and life challenges.

The resources and techniques that I have outlined here are meant to help you manage symptoms and behaviors. This book is not meant to be a substitute for psychotherapy. If you find that your symptoms require more than what is provided here, please seek treatment. In order to clear the roots of your problems, I recommend EMDR, one of the most powerful and effective therapies available today. EMDR works well for post-traumatic stress disorder, as well as other trauma-based problems that cause a myriad of symptoms, including relationship difficulties, anxiety disorders, depression, substance abuse, low self-esteem, and blocks to creativity and self-expression. Find a therapist who is certified in EMDR in your area. For more information on EMDR I refer you to my book *Transforming Trauma: EMDR*.

In closing, I want to wish you all the best on your healing journey. Remember, you have all the resources you need within yourself. Use your imagination and your two hands to unlock the power of these resources and put them to work.

ACKNOWLEDGMENTS

MY HEARTFELT APPRECIATION goes out to my family and friends who have accompanied me on this writing path for some time. I want to thank Pierre Blais, my beloved husband, whose love and support deeply nourishes me. Thank you to my sons, Catono Perez and Etienne Perez-Parnell, who are always in my heart. My appreciation to Nischala Devi, fellow teacher and writer, for her precious friendship, tender love, and useful feedback on the manuscript. My special thanks to John Prendergast, who helped me formulate the basic principles of resource tapping and provided helpful advice along the way. Thank you to Joan (Alonnsi) Ruvinsky, whose enthusiasm for the book and technique was very encouraging. She demonstrated that resource tapping could be used successfully to help anxious yoga students. Thank you to Dina Tarah for her wise counsel and helpful ideas. My appreciation to Jean Pumphrey, dear friend, aunt, mentor, and poet, who was my first and best writing teacher.

Thank you to my mother, Helen McDonald, who helped give me a well-resourced childhood enabling me to grow and flourish as an adult and to my father, Dean Parnell, and step-mother, Sue Parnell. I want to pay tribute to my wonderful, loving grandparents Ray and Florence James, who provided for me emotionally as well as financially. I carry inside me always sweet memories of times with them as sources of comfort and well-being.

Many thanks to Francine Shapiro for her tireless work in the development and advancement of EMDR, which has helped countless traumatized people the world over, and for her early work with resource installation upon which resource tapping has grown. My appreciation to the EMDR therapists who have helped in the development of EMDR and resource tapping, some of whom contributed case material for this book: Alison Teal, Harriet Sage, Linda Cohn, Susan Tieger, Cynthia Kong, Caryn Markson, Landry Wildwind, Nancy Bravman, Debbe Davis and Marsha Sage. Thank you to A. J. Popky for his contribution to the treatment of addictions with resource (installation) tapping and to Sandra (Sam) Foster and Jennifer Lendl for their work with performance enhancement, to Andrew Leeds for his resource installation protocol. Thank you to Alison Teal for her contribution to the use of resource tapping for healing from injury. Many thanks to my German friends Christa Diegelmann and Margarete Isermann, who have inspired me with their resource tapping work with cancer patients and supplied me with additional resource ideas. My appreciation to all the clients whose stories have been included in this book.

Thank you to Maggie Phillips, a leader in the field of trauma therapy and pain treatment, who taught me the body safe place and other somatic techniques. My appreciation to Peter Levine for planting the seeds for this book at Esalen, and for his pioneering and inspiring work with traumatized people. I want to acknowledge Jean Klein as one of the sources for healing injury and illness using body sensing. Many of the principles and ideas originate from his teaching.

My appreciation to Sheryl Fullerton, my former agent, who has continued to help me negotiate in the world of publishing. Thank you to the wonderful staff at Sounds True, who truly practice and live what they present to the world. I feel deeply fortunate to be working with this excellent team of professionals. My appreciation to Jennifer Coffee for recognizing the importance of this healing technique and shepherding the project from beginning to end with grace and good humor. Thank you to Andrew Merz for his help shaping and editing the manuscript and to Kelly Notaras for her editing and polishing. My appreciation to Mitchell Clute and the recording production team at Sounds True, who made me comfortable and at home in the recording studio.

Words cannot express the gratitude I feel for my spiritual mentors and teachers. Joseph Goldstein, Jack Kornfield, and Sharon Salzberg were early and important influences who taught me Vipassana meditation. My appreciation to Suzanne Segal, psychologist, mentor and friend, whose spiritual awakening helped many of us recognize this same freedom in ourselves. To my spiritual teachers, no longer in physical form, but living forever in my heart, Lama Thubten Yeshe and Jean Klein, my deep appreciation for all that they gave me through their teachings and living example. Like spiritual parents, they tenderly guided me to my Self. Finally, I thank His Holiness the Dalai Lama for his wise and compassionate teachings and his luminous presence.

Complete List of
Resources in This Book

Resources for Comfort

Love Resources

Resources for Peace and Calm

Resources for Empowerment

Uplifting Resources

Spiritual and Wisdom Resources

Resources for Healing, Illness, and Trauma

EMDR INFORMATION

EMDR INTERNATIONAL ASSOCIATION (EMDRIA)

The EMDR International Association is a non-profit professional membership organization that approves trainings and certifies therapists, consultants, and trainers in EMDR. EMDRIA has information about EMDR trainings and workshops as well as referrals to EMDR-trained therapists. This is a good source for information on EMDR. **www.emdria.org**

HUMANITARIAN ASSISTANCE PROGRAM (HAP)

This non-profit organization helps people all over the world recover from trauma by providing pro-bono or low cost EMDR training to local professionals as well as direct service to traumatized communities. **www.emdrhap.org**

ABOUT THE AUTHOR

A psychologist, teacher, and author with over thirty years experience as a meditator and spiritual practitioner, LAUREL PARNELL, PH.D. has actively integrated psychological and spiritual work throughout her career. She served on the faculty of the California Institute for Integral Studies and John F. Kennedy University and presents at conferences in the United States and abroad. An innovator and expert in EMDR (Eye Movement Desensitization and Reprocessing) she has trained thousands of clinicians in the United States and abroad. Her books include *Transforming Trauma: EMDR,*

EMDR in the Treatment of Adults Abused as Children and *A Therapist's Guide to EMDR*. She leads workshops and trainings in resource tapping and EMDR throughout the world. She maintains a private practice in San Rafael, California.

Please visit www.emdrinfo.com for information about world-wide trainings and workshops in EMDR and resource tapping with Dr. Parnell.

ALSO BY SOUNDS TRUE

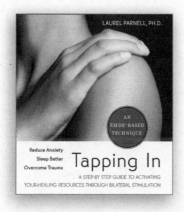

Tapping In
A STEP-BY-STEP GUIDE TO ACTIVATING
YOUR HEALING RESOURCES THROUGH
BILATERAL STIMULATION

Dr. Laurel Parnell presents two CDs of instruction for
learning the core practices of resource tapping to release
anxiety, build resilience, calm the body, and more.

U.S. $19.95 / ISBN 978-1-59179-810-1

To order or request more information,
call 800-333-9185 or visit www.soundstrue.com.

ABOUT SOUNDS TRUE

SOUNDS TRUE was founded in 1985 with a clear vision: to disseminate spiritual wisdom. Located in Boulder, Colorado, Sounds True publishes teaching programs that are designed to educate, uplift, and inspire. We work with many of the leading spiritual teachers, thinkers, healers, and visionary artists of our time.

To receive a free catalog of tools and teachings for personal and spiritual transformation, please visit www.soundstrue.com, call toll-free 800-333-9185, or write to us at the address below.

The Sounds True Catalog
PO Box 8010
Boulder, CO 80306